Book of Sun and Moon
(I Ching)

日月經

Traditional Perspectives on Divination and Calculation
for the *Book of Changes* (Volume I)

Translation and Commentaries
by Stuart Alve Olson

Valley Spirit Arts
Phoenix, Arizona

Copyright © 2014 by Stuart Alve Olson.

All rights reserved. No part of this publication may be reproduced or used in any form or by any means, electronic or mechanical, including photocopying, recording, or by any information storage and retrieval system, without prior written permission from Stuart Alve Olson and Valley Spirit Arts LLC.

ISBN-13: 978-1-5032-9093-8
ISBN-10: 1-5032-9093-X

Valley Spirit Arts
Phoenix, Arizona
www.valleyspiritarts.com
contact@valleyspiritarts.com

Editing, book design, and graphics by Patrick Gross.

Fu Xi (circa 2852 BCE) is one the Four Great Sages of the *Book of Sun and Moon*. He is credited with creating the Eight Trigrams and assigning correlations to them.

The highest tranquility of the Dao cannot be adapted to any type of uniform calculation, but there are strangely wonderful vessels in which the Ten Thousand Things are brought forth, such as the Eight Diagrams, the Sexagenary Cycles, the Spirits, Root Powers, and the Hidden Ghosts.

These are the mysteries of mutual empowerment of the Yin and Yang, which advances and makes these images clear to all.

The Yellow Emperor's Yin Convergence Scripture
(黃帝陰符經, *Huang Di Yin Fu Jing*)

Acknowledgments

In 1967 the karmic seeds for this book were first planted. As a birthday present, a friend gave me a copy of *The I Ching, or, Book of Changes* by Wilhelm and Baynes. Since I had been reading works by Tuesday Lopsang Rampa at the time, she must have thought this translated Chinese book would be of interest to me. She was right, but truthfully I had no idea what the *Book of Changes* was getting at. I loved all the sayings, but had no intelligent conception of any of it. It just seemed cool to me. Back then I had no idea how influential and intrinsic this book would become to my life. So I must begin this acknowledgement with deep gratitude to my friend and to Richard Wilhelm and Cary F. Baynes.

Many years later, in 1979, while living at the City of Ten Thousand Buddhas in Ukiah, California, I found out that the abbott, Chan Master Hsuan Hua, had memorized the *Book of Changes* earlier in his life, and so I set about doing the same. In one of his lectures, Master Hua said something that greatly influenced me, "If you memorize something, it is yours," which has proven really true. Also, while living there I was fortunate enough to sit in on the *Book of Changes* classes of Prof. Thomas Lin, and of Prof. Wu Yi, a resident philosophy teacher for the Dharma Realm Buddhist University. Both of these learned men really helped me develop insights into the *Book of Changes* that I never would have received elsewhere—my deepest gratitude to them.

In 1980 I undertook the task of translating the entire *Book of Changes* and its associated *Ten Wings*. Since that time I have played with the idea of publishing the work, but so many other projects prevented me from doing so. From 1982 until his death in 2002, Master T.T. Liang helped make many corrections to my translations, for which I am deeply indebted to him.

In 1993 I formed a friendship with Prof. Koon Yuipoon, who was extremely helpful in showing me insights into the uses of the *Book of Changes* and fine tuning my translation, and he presented me with some very insightful Chinese texts on the *Book of Changes*. I am also deeply indebted to him for his contributions.

During the many years I've read, studied, and used the *Book of Changes*, I've always found it to speak truth to me, even though it wasn't always apparent at first examination. I kept studying it, however, and researched many good books in Chinese on the subject.

In 1995, I printed my initial translation of the work for a group of students who were taking a month-long workshop I was conducting at the Institute of Internal Arts in St. Paul, Minnesota.

Over the next dozen years I simply kept studying and applying the *Book of Changes* to my daily life. In 2008, while living in Phoenix, Arizona, I led an in-depth workshop on the *Book of Changes,* and from that an ongoing weekly class developed. Many students were very helpful in encouraging me to elucidate various aspects of the *Book of Changes,* which then led to this present series of books.

To all of them, I offer my deepest gratitude: Lily Shank, Patrick Gross, Prof. Dave Capco, Marguerite Mullins, Amy Searcy, Jason Campbell, Michael Leonie, Beth Leonie, Fred and Julie Werner. Without them, the *Book of Sun and Moon* may not have ever been written, and most likely would have just remained scattered thoughts in my head and various files in my computer. My most heartfelt appreciation to all of them.

Lastly, I must give special thanks to Patrick Gross who has worked on countless drafts of this work, designed and created the many graphics, and kept after me to make it more clear. To my wife, Lily, who likewise was relentless in her pursuit of encouraging me to get these books done. Alas! They both achieved their goal. I bow to them.

Contents

Introduction 1
   The Sun and Moon Connection 3
   The Purpose of This Work 8
   Conclusion 10

Part One: Sages of the *Book of Sun and Moon* 11
   Fu Xi 11
   Yu the Great 12
   King Wen 13
   Duke of Zhou 14
   Confucius 15
   Wang Bi 16
   Shao Yong 17
   Zhou Dunyi 18
   Daoist Alchemical and Cosmology Masters 19
      Wei Boyang 19
      Zhang Boduan 19
      Liu Yiming 20

Part Two: History of the *Book of Sun and Moon* 21
   The Three *Yi* Books 21
   The *Original Yi* and *Modern Yi* 21
   Ten Wings 22
   Upper and *Lower Books* of the *Yi* 24

Part Three: Formation of the Trigrams and Hexagrams 31
   The Three Powers in the Trigrams and Hexagrams 35

Part Four: The Eight Trigram Arrangements 37
   Original Before Heaven Arrangement 38
   Newer Before Heaven Arrangement 39
   Contrasted Image Arrangement 40
   Eight Gates Arrangement 42
   After Heaven Arrangement 43

Part Five: The Eight Houses of the Sixty-Four Hexagrams 49
- The Eight Houses of the Before Heaven Arrangement of Hexagrams 49
- The Eight Houses of the Contrasted Image Arrangement of Hexagrams 52
- The Eight Houses of the Eight Gates Arrangement of Hexagrams 54
- The Eight Houses of the After Heaven Arrangement of Hexagrams 57

Part Six: Numerological Calculations of the Yi 61
- Ho River Map and Lo River Script 61
- The Nine Palaces 68
- The Sexagenary Cycles 73
- The Twelve Palaces 75
- The Sixty-Year Cycle of Hexagrams 76
- Ruling Lines 80
- Sovereign Hexagrams of the Calendar 80
- The Eight Positions of the Before Heaven and After Heaven Arrangements in Correlation with the Supreme Ultimate Symbol 82

Part Seven: Using the *Book of Sun and Moon* 85
- The Prediction and Lines 86
- Great Symbolism 86
- Trigram Correlations 87
  - The Eight Nei Dan Qi Centers 88
  - The Eight Extraordinary Nei Dan Meridians/Vessels 88
  - The Eight Wai Dan Qi Meridians 91
- The Twenty-Eight Mansions 95
- Associated Developed Hexagrams From Casting 100
- Examples of Traditional Methods of Triangulation 106
- Example for Interpreting a Casted Before Heaven Hexagram 112
- The Eight Houses 115
- Changing Lines 121

Part Eight: Casting the Stalks and Ritual for Divination 123
- Daoist Ritual for Casting the Stalks 123
- Purifying the Altar Chant 124
- The Stalks for Divining 126

Suggested Reading 131
About the Author 133
Chart for Determining Hexagrams 136

Introduction

The *Book of Sun and Moon* (易經, *Yi Jing*), more popularly known as the *Book of Changes*, is not only one of the oldest surviving literary works in the world, it remains one of the most profound pieces of literature ever composed. As a foundational work of Chinese culture, the *Book of Sun and Moon* serves as a book of wisdom, divination, cosmology, calculation, philosophy, imagery, science, internal alchemy, and a means to map all phenomena. The full scope and importance of this work should not be underestimated. It is, on one hand, a simple work, yet equally so complex that some of the greatest minds in Chinese history never completely grasped all its complexities.

These volumes on the *Book of Sun and Moon* present, in my opinion, the most important tools and information on how to utilize the *Yi Jing*. The *Book of Sun and Moon,* an alternative—though accurate—translation for the title of the *Yi Jing,* is both a book of divination and calculation. Its use in divination means to apply intuition concerning the oracle of the hexagrams (the sixty-four images of broken and unbroken Yin-and-Yang lines). Its ability to calculate and determine possible outcomes for any situation involves examining the logical correlations associated with each of the hexagrams and what images they change into and head toward. So to simply translate the *Yi Jing* without presenting the associated numerological and image-based logic only serves to limit those who seek to interpret the *Book of Sun and Moon* in the most accurate and complete sense.

Using the *Book of Sun and Moon* is like being a detective or tracker. The images are the clues and tracks, and a good detective or tracker needs not only tools of deduction and observation, but also a strong sense of intuition. Hence, the *Book of Sun and Moon* provides the main tools for both.

Some questions put to the *Book of Sun and Moon* may only seem to need an understanding of just the oracle portion (presented in volume II)—meaning, to use your intuition. Others require the use of logic and calculation. Without the ability to apply both intuition and logic, however, you are only receiving half the picture and limiting the amount of information the *Book of Sun and Moon* can provide.

In *A Collection on the Essentials of the Rivers He and Luo* (河洛精蘊, *He Lou Jing Yun)*, it states,

> The ancient *Yi* is a book of divination and calculation. Its use is to know the past and to know the future so to attain sagely wisdom.
> 古易是卜筮而推算之書. 知往知來用得聖慧.
> Gu Yi Shi Bu Shi Er Tui Suan Zhi Shu. Zhi Wang Zhi Lai Yong De Sheng Hui.

In chapter 3 of the *Treatise of Remarks on the Trigrams* (說卦傳, *Shuo Gua Zhuan*) of the *Ten Wings* (十翼, *Shi Yi*), it states,

> Calculation of the past is a natural process, having foreknowledge is to foresee [intuition]. Therefore, the *Yi* is used for both calculation and foreseeing.
> 數往者順, 知來者逆. 是故易逆數也.
> Shu Wang Zhe Shun, Zhi Lai Zhe Ni. Shi Gu *Yi* Ni Shu Ye.

The *Book of Sun and Moon* is unquestionably the first computerlike code created. Instead of using the values of zeros and ones to create images on our computer screens, the *Book of Sun and Moon* uses *Yin* (broken lines or black dots) and *Yang* (unbroken lines or white dots) to accomplish the same thing—an image. The sixty-four six-lined hexagrams of broken and unbroken lines has 11,250 variations, and if considering the many possible ways of interpreting each variation, an almost infinite number of permutations can occur. The *Book of Sun and Moon* at its core is mathematical, and math, without question, is a universal language. In the case of the *Book of Sun and Moon*, the functions of math, imagery, and intuition are equally being used, which puts this work into a category far beyond mere literature and science. I can think of no other book that encompasses such vast territory in function, purpose, and meaning. Confucius, a prolific writer on the *Book of Sun and Moon*, deeply regretted that he could not have another fifty years of life to continue his studies of the *Yi Jing*.

The *Book of Sun and Moon*, when first written, dates back approximately three thousand years, and if we accept the postulation that the theories of trigrams were formed nearly three thousand years before King Wen, then we are looking at a system of divination and calculation nearly six thousand years old. Surely the *Book of Sun and Moon* has surpassed the test of time far greater than any other piece of literature.

Before King Wen's time, the class of divination experts called Fang Shi (方師), which translates as "Method Masters" and/or "Direction Masters," held great power and influence. Going back to the Xia dynasty (夏朝, Xia Chao, 2070 to 1600 BCE) and the Shang dynasty (商朝, Shang Chao, 1600 to 1046 BCE) archeologists were finding examples of the tortoise shells and ox bones that the Fang Shi heated until cracks appeared, which they then interpreted to foretell coming events. The Fang Shi, for the most part, were advisors to the rulers and aristocrats of their time, so it was not a practice of the common people. In many ways, Fang Shi carried the same positions and roles modern-day lawyers, consultants, and aides serve for politicians and businesses.

Despite the discoveries of tortoise shells and ox bones being used for divination, little information exists on how the cracks were interpreted. The actual method for divination and interpretation of images did not happen until sometime in the Zhou dynasty (周朝, Zhou Chao, 1046 to 256 BCE) when King Wen is said to have revised the method for casting images. His writings, forming the original *Book of Sun and Moon,* and use of yarrow stalks to reveal the Yin and Yang images of trigrams and hexagrams effectively ended the use of plastromancy (using a hot poker to create cracks on the undersurface of a hollowed out tortoise shell) and scapulimancy (the practice of reading ox shoulder bones, wherein a knife was used to scrape away the outer surface of the bone which was then heated to produce cracks). The use of tortoise shells and ox bones predated King Wen's methods by hundreds of years, but no actual text for the *Book of Sun and Moon* appeared until the Zhou dynasty, so it is uncertain how the cracks were actually interpreted. Interestingly, tortoise shells and ox bones have provided some of the earliest examples of Chinese writing.

When it comes to the history and use of the methods and principles of the *Book of Sun and Moon,* nothing can accurately be dated before King Wen's time. The methods for deriving a hexagram for interpretation have been varied, beginning with the use of tortoise shells, then ox bones, and at some point during the Zhou dynasty, yarrow stalks became the accepted method. Later, coins, bamboo slips, Yin-Yang wood blocks, and presently computers are being employed. How the ancients, pre-Zhou dynasty, interpreted the cracks in tortoise shells and ox bones remains a mystery. Even concerning the actual text of the *Book of Changes,* the history is quite cloudy. The *Ma Wang Dui* manuscript discovered in present times, which dates back to 168 BCE, is substantially identical to the present version, but the hexagrams are in a different order. The current text was structured in the second century BCE, and was taken as the standard arrangement by Wang Bi (226–249 CE).

The Sun and Moon Connection

Even the character *Yi* (易) offers insights into the depth of the work, and is one of the reasons this present book is titled the *Book of Sun and Moon* instead of one of the more common translations of *Book of Changes, Book of Zhou* (周經, *Zhou Jing*), or *Zhou Dynasty Book of Change* (周易, *Zhou Yi*). The use of *Sun and Moon* in the title comes from the two radicals that comprise the ideogram *Yi* (易). *Ri* (日), the upper radical, translates as the "Sun," and *Wu* (勿), the bottom radical, is an older variant of *Yue* (月), the "Moon." Therefore, *Yi* is an ideogram denoting the Sun and Moon, or better said, "the constant interchange of movements of the Sun and Moon."

The actual derivation of the ideogram *Yi* (易) meant a "chameleon," a lizard able to easily change colors according to its environment. From this usage, *Yi* came to mean "change" and "easy." The chameleon, an Earthly relative of the more celestial Dragon in Chinese thought, was symbolic of how the Sun and Moon likewise changes in brightness and darkness, a Yin and Yang interchange. The ideogram for *Yang* (陽) is described as the sunny side of a hill (the south side), and *Yin* (陰), the dark side of a hill (north). Thus, these two ideograms likewise express the idea of an interchange of brightness and darkness. In summation, King Wen's adaptation of the character *Yi* was absolutely brilliant in the context of expressing these ideas of *Sun* and *Moon*, *Yin* and *Yang*, *solar* and *lunar*, *celestial* and *terrestrial*, *changing* and *unchanging*, *light* and *dark*, and so on, all in one ideogram.

As noted, the character *Yi* can mean "easy," and it may also be that King Wen was indicating the *Yi* to mean *The Book of Easy*. This is a possible interpretation because King Wen had transposed a very complex system into an easier one by revising the Ho River Map and Lo River Script diagrams—a series of white and black dots—into the pattern of Eight Trigram (八卦, Ba Gua) images, and then stacking them upon each other to create the Sixty-Four Hexagrams to complete the *Book of Sun and Moon*. Without question, stacking trigrams to form an image is far easier than attempting to stack the white and black dots of the Ho River Map and Lo River Script. In this light, the *Book of Easy* is quite an appropriate title.

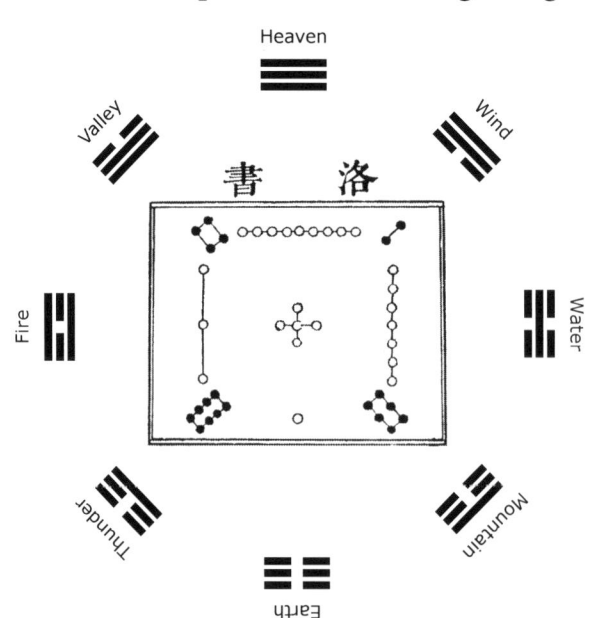

The Lo River Script and Correlated Eight Trigrams

The Eight Trigrams of Heaven ☰ and Earth ☷, Fire ☲ and Water ☵, Valley ☱ and Mountain ☶, and Thunder ☳ and Wind ☴ are the trigrams (three-lined symbols) used in the *Book of Sun and Moon* for determining the changes that occur in the Heavenly, Earthly, and Humanly realms, called the *Three Powers* (三才, *San Cai*)— acting as a visual imagery indicator of past, present, and future conditions and events. Several correlations to the Sun and Moon are found within the trigrams. For example, the trigram for Heaven ☰ (乾, Qian) is associated with and revealed by the trigram of Fire ☲ (離, Li), the Sun. The trigram for Earth ☷ (坤, Kun) is associated and revealed by the trigram for Water ☵ (坎, Kan), the Moon.

As seen above, the trigram Valley ☱ (兌, Dui) is being translated as "Valley" rather than the standard "Lake," "Rivers," or "Marsh" as found in other works. This is because all water flows into the low places, or valleys. Also, the other trigrams all have a logical contrasted representation, or complementary opposite. Heaven pairs with and is contrasted by Earth, Fire with Water, Thunder/Lightning with Wind/Rain. All these images logically contrast with and complement each other. "Marsh," "Lake," or "Rivers" doesn't pair up with "Mountain" in the same way. The opposite of a Mountain is a Valley, and it is into valleys that all things flow or are collected, not just water, but wind as well. Valleys are the passes in which to travel through the mountains. The ideogram *Dui* means to "open up" in the context of a path or pass. It also carries the meaning "to permeate," as something that infuses and goes into something else.

The notion of a "marsh" and "lake" was first presented by Confucius in the *Great Symbolism* section of the *Ten Wings*, not by King Wen or Duke of Zhou. It can only be assumed that King Wen in using the ideogram *Dui* (兌) did so with the original meaning in mind, wherein it shows a person walking through a valley or ravine.

In Confucius's defense, he didn't actually use the ideogram *Dui* to mean a marsh or lake, he used an alternative ideogram to do so in the *Great Symbolism*. For example, in the *Great Symbolism* of *Dui* ䷹, the 58th hexagram, he wrote, "Connected Marshes. This is Dui." For the idea of marshes, he uses the ideogram *Ze* (澤). So, in this context, Confucius himself didn't view the term *Dui* purely as a lake or marsh.

Sun and Moon Within the Tai Ji Symbol

Within the Tai Ji Symbol created by Zhou Dunyi (周敦頤, 1017 to 1073 CE), the idea of *Yin within Yang,* and *Yang within Yin* can clearly be seen. This diagram could equally be interpreted as *Water within Heaven,* and *Fire within Earth.* Hence, when putting the Eight Trigrams around the Supreme Ultimate Symbol (太極圖, Tai Ji Tu) the small black circle is represented by the image of Kan ☵ (Water), and the small white circle is representing the image of Li ☲ (Fire).

Fire ☲ is equated to the sunlight and warmth the Earth receives, and Water ☵ represents the influences of the bodies of water and of the Moon on Earth (such as the ocean tides and the influences upon tides by the eight phases of the Moon). Heaven ☰ and Earth ☷, therefore, are considered the "cosmic" or "celestial" representations of Sun and Moon, symbolized in the ideogram *Yi* (易). Fire ☲ and Water ☵ represent the earthly/humanly aspects of Sun and Moon, symbolized in the ideogram *Ming* (明)— meaning "illumination," "clarity," or "wisdom"—which is also made up of the two ideograms for Sun (日) and Moon (月).

Apart from the ideograms and trigram associations for Sun and Moon, using the title *Book of Sun and Moon* is really nothing new, as even in the *Ten Wings* (Confucian commentaries on the *Yi*) there appears an explanation of this Sun and Moon correlation.

In chapter 5 of the *Lower Appendix* (繫辭下傳, *Xi Ci Xia Zhuan*) of the *Ten Wings*, it says,

> The Sun departs and then the Moon arrives. The Moon departs and then the Sun arrives. The Sun and Moon each take the other's place, and so their illumination is created.
> 日往則月來, 月往則日來, 日月相推而明生焉.
> Ri Wang Wang Ze Yue Lai, Yue Wang Ze Ri Lai, Ri Yue Xiang Tui Er Ming Sheng Yan.

So it is with the images in the *Yi*, when a Sun (hexagram) image is complete, its reflected or opposite Moon image appears. Within the *Ten Wings* there are numerous references to the Sun and Moon, so this dual relationship of the Sun and Moon is not out of context for this work.

Even though *Yi* can mean "change" and "easy," the Sixty-Four Hexagrams in the book are based on the functions of the Sun and Moon. For example, examining hexagram #3 *Difficult Beginnings* ䷂ (純, Chun),[1] along with its Moon image of #4 *Untaught Youth* ䷃ (蒙, Meng), it can be seen how #4 ䷃ is just a reversed reflection of #3 ䷂—meaning, turn #3 ䷂ upside down and you will see #4 ䷃. For the most part in the *Book of Sun and Moon*, the odd-numbered hexagrams are Yang (or Sun), and the even-numbered ones are Yin (or Moon). The even-numbered hexagrams are, in almost all cases, a reflected reverse image of their preceding odd-numbered counterpart. The principle here is that the Moon can only be viewed when it is reflecting the light of the Sun. Hence, #4 ䷃ can only be produced because of the formation of #3 ䷂.

This progression of Sun and Moon images are applicable within sixty of the Sixty-Four Hexagrams. Four hexagrams—#1 ䷀ and #2 ䷁, as well as #29 ䷜ and #30 ䷝—are direct contrasted (or opposite) images of each other, and in the *Yi* serve as the "Four Pillars" that frame the *Upper Book*. Hexagrams #27 ䷚ and #28 ䷛ of the *Upper Book*, and #61 ䷼ and #62 ䷽ of the *Lower Book* act as eclipses of the Sun and Moon. (These distinctions will be explained in greater detail in a forthcoming work titled *The Logic of the Formation of the Sixty-Four Hexagrams*.)

---

[1] Note that hexagrams designated as "Sun" appear in this lighter shade: ䷂. "Moon" hexagrams are shown in black: ䷃.

One other aspect of this Sun and Moon relationship in the *Book of Sun and Moon* needs clarification. Hexagrams #29 ䷜ and #30 ䷝, and #63 ䷾ and #64 ䷿, are reversed in their Sun and Moon positions, as are the Ecliptic Hexagrams (#27 ䷚ and #28 ䷛, and #61 ䷼ and #62 ䷽). Image #29 ䷜, *The Abyss,* contains the two trigrams of Water, and Water belongs in the West (the Yin, or Moon, side of the Eight Trigrams). Image #30 ䷝, *Distant Brightness,* contains the two trigrams of Fire, and Fire belongs in the East (the Yang, or Sun, side of the Eight Trigrams).

The Purpose of This Work

This translation of the *Book of Sun and Moon* focuses on three main goals:

1) To reinstitute the theories and practices of the early Chinese School of Image and Numerological Studies (象數學, Xiang Shu Xue) of the *Book of Sun and Moon,* rather than the predominant school drawing from Confucianism—Principles of Righteousness Studies (義理學, Yi Li Xue). The *Book of Sun and Moon,* as it has been transmitted through the generations, has been to a greater extent a springboard for Confucian philosophy. The *Ten Wings* are very much evidence of this approach, whereas the teachings of Shao Yong and Zhou Dunyi (Image and Numerological Studies) have not received as much attention.

2) To provide more insight and clarity to the Before Heaven, Contrasted Image, Eight Gates, and After Heaven arrangements of the Sixty-Four Hexagrams, as the intents and purposes of these arrangements have long been avoided or left in obscurity by many writers and translators of the *Yi Jing*.

3) To be a source book for the future companion work *The Logic of the Formation of the Sixty-Four Hexagrams*. Although many English books on the *Book of Changes* are available, few deal with its structural aspects, or question the translations of not only the title (such as using "Sun and Moon" rather than "Changes"), or look at the associations with the trigrams, or provide any logic as to why the hexagrams are not just a random selection of images and, in doing so, take some of the mystery out of the After Heaven Arrangement.

These ways of looking at the *Book of Sun and Moon* may seem new or different when compared to the typical books currently translated and published in English, but the material presented in this work originates from traditional perspectives and insights into the *Book of Sun and Moon* that are available in various Chinese sources, if one is willing to do the research. This book is the first in a series of works on the *Book of Sun and Moon* that comes from my more than forty years of examining this wonderful text and piecing together often cryptic information, commentaries, and insights into the *Book of Sun and Moon* by many great teachers, scholars, and Daoist masters.

Apart from the above purposes, this book also presents several old diagrams and graphics used to define and illustrate various aspects of the *Book of Sun and Moon,* acting as source materials for much of the work. Equally, many new graphics and diagrams were designed for this work, as the originals were either too faded or poorly drawn. The *Book of Sun and Moon,* in its deepest sense, is a book of imagery, and the words attached to the images are not the heart of this work. Therefore, learning how to interpret the trigrams and hexagrams from a casting, and their role in developing one's intuition, is of the greatest importance. Images within the human consciousness have a much more profound and deeper meaning than words could ever express. Words are indeed helpful, but it is the imagery and intuition one perceives from the hexagrams that are the essence of the *Book of Sun and Moon.*

Keep in mind that the way of interpreting a hexagram as presented by Confucian philosophy is only partially correct. Seeing hexagram #14, *Great Possession,* for example, as just Fire over Heaven represents only one viewpoint. This hexagram could equally be viewed as Heaven ascending to Fire, as Fire within Heaven, or as Fire reflecting Heaven. It wasn't King Wen who adhered to this sole idea of looking at this hexagram as just Fire over Heaven, a claim he never made in *The Prediction* (彖, Tuan), his explanation of the hexagrams. To fully interpret and understand the hexagram images, one has to examine them from many angles and not be limited by rote views of them. Hence, this work attempts to provide several manners in which to interpret the hexagrams, and therefore strengthen and expand your intuition. In *The Yellow Emperor's Yin Convergence Scripture* it states,

Ignorant people study the principles of Heaven and Earth to become a sage.
I study the principles of the seasons and the affairs and phenomena of the world to become intuitive.
愚人以天地文理聖, 我以時物文理哲.
Yu Ren Yi TIan Di Wen Li Sheng, Wo Yi Shi Wu Wen Li Zhe.

This verse goes to the very heart of how the *Book of Sun and Moon* should be approached and cultivated. The development of the intuition is far superior to that of reading and studying "principles of Heaven and Earth" (a reference to studying the Confucian classics). Rather by studying Nature (the seasons and workings of Nature) we develop our intuition. The *Book of Sun and Moon* is based on the workings of Nature and, therefore, is a conduit for developing the intuition.

The above statement also brings up one of the foundational bases of the *Book of Sun and Moon,* which functions and is derived from the movements of the Sun, Moon, and constellations. There were no clocks in King Wen's time, so people back then paid attention to Moon phases, seasonal changes, solar changes, and constellation movements. Very few people nowadays follow these constructs of time, rather just relying on clocks and calendars, which, though convenient, render no means for developing a person's intuition about Nature.

Conclusion

The following sections are meant to take the reader through many of the important aspects of the *Book of Sun and Moon.* Even though I cannot explain the full historical development of all the associations and correlations presented, I have tried my best to make them understandable, especially in the context of how they relate to the *Book of Sun and Moon (Yi Jing).*

The enormity of history and developments of the *Book of Sun and Moon* over China's long history is far beyond the scope of this work, and of any other books on this subject. It so vast and deep that I feel humbled in even presenting this work. This is akin to explaining a couple of stars in the night sky, not an explanation of the cosmos. These volumes on the *Book of Sun and Moon,* likewise, are not definitive works, rather they explain various aspects of the *Yi Jing's* developments and uses. The *Yi Jing* is at the root of many aspects particular to Chinese culture, and it greatly influenced the development of China's two indigenous philosophies of Daoism (道教, Dao Jiao) and Confucianism (儒教, Ru Jiao), as well as the arts of Feng Shui, Taijiquan, Chinese numerology, medicine, astrology, and the Chinese calendar. It is without question as influential as Lao Zi's *Scripture on the Way and Virtue* (道德經, Dao De Jing), if not more so, because the *Yi Jing (Book of Sun and Moon)* extends into so many facets of Chinese culture, and its roots go back to the very beginnings of Chinese civilization.

—Stuart Alve Olson
Autumn 2014

Part One

Sages of the Book of Sun and Moon

The following material provides brief biographies of the major figures connected to the formation of the *Book of Sun and Moon*. Despite its brevity, this section covers a time span (over four thousand years of history) of various developments of the *Book of Sun and Moon*. Few records are as confusing as the history of the *Book of Sun and Moon*. The differing fables, wild history, and lack of concise historical data makes it near impossible, in any practical sense, to know who created what and when. The simple history presented here is in many ways just a glimpse at the figures who, at least in the popular sense, contributed to the formation of the *Yi* as we presently study and use it today.

Before giving descriptions of the following sages and assigning their contributions to the formation of the *Book of Sun and Moon,* a few critical observations must be mentioned. First, there are no records from King Wen's hand describing why the Sixty-Four Hexagrams appear in the order they are commonly given or even if it was he who actually arranged them this way. King Wen never mentions trigrams, nor is there any actual evidence he created the After Heaven images, in either the Eight Trigram form or of all Sixty-Four Hexagrams. All of this is conjecture. Trigrams were first mentioned by Confucius in his *Great Symbolism* within the *Ten Wings*. The actual construction of the Eight Houses, both in the Before Heaven and After Heaven constructs, seems not to have appeared until the time of Shao Yong in the Song dynasty (960–1279 CE).

Fu Xi (伏羲), or Bao Xi (包犧)

Fu Xi (circa 2852 BCE) is the first of the five legendary emperors of China. Although no historical documents have proven his existence, persistent folklore legends record him as the inventor of agriculture and writing, and as the creator of the Eight Trigrams. In the commentaries of the *Ten Wings* he is referred to as Bao Xi and is considered one the Four Great Sages of the *Book of Sun and Moon* by Confucians. In these commentaries he is credited with creating the trigrams and assigning correlations to them.

Chapter 2 of the *Lower Appendix* of the *Ten Wings* provides the following depiction of Fu Xi's role in the creation of the *Yi*:

> In antiquity, when Bao Xi came to rule everything under Heaven, he looked up into the sky and saw all the exhibitions of the bright forms. When he looked down he could survey all the various patterns on the Earth. Then he contemplated the appearances of all the various birds and beasts, and all the different soils. Things near and things of his own person, and things distant and all things in general, he pondered them all. It was from these observations he first devised the Eight Images [Trigrams].
>
> 古者包犧氏之王天下也. 仰則觀象於天. 俯則觀法於地. 觀鳥獸之文. 與地之宜. 近取諸身. 遠取諸物. 於是始作八卦.
>
> Gu Zhe Bao Xi Shi Zhi Wang Tian Xia Ye. Yang Ze Guan Xiang Yu Tian. Fu Ze Guan Fa Yu Di. Guan Niao Shou Zhi Wen. Yu Di Zhi Yi. Jin Qu Zhu Shen. Yuan Qu Zhu Wu. Yu Shi Shi Zuo Ba Gua.

What is interesting about this quote is that it gives no mention of the common story of Fu Xi seeing a tortoise crawl out of the Yellow River with the Eight Trigram markings on its shell. What is plausible is that Fu Xi designated eight emblematic signs, celestial and terrestrial, in nature for Heaven and Earth, Valleys and Mountains, Fire and Water, and Thunder/Lightning and Wind/Rain—which collectively exhibit the very primal essences and constructs of all phenomena and functions of Nature.

Yu the Great (大禹, Da Yu), or Xia Yu (夏禹)

In the legends of Yu the Great (circa 2205 BCE, another of the five legendary emperors of China) appear folklore accounts of him seeing a tortoise coming out of the Yellow River with markings on its shell. He is also credited with inventing the Ho River Map and the Lo River Script (河圖洛書, Ho Tu Lo Shu), and these are considered the origins of both the Before Heaven and After Heaven arrangements of the Eight Trigrams. Because of the black and white circles, these charts appear more as emblems of constellations. Even so, these two diagrams did come to represent the two Eight Trigram arrangements and they are also the founding patterns for the numbering system in the numerological divination method of the Nine Palaces Diagram (see p. 69).

Yu the Great is normally referred to as the God of Wind and Water (風水, Feng Shui), as legends of him relate that he devised the means for stopping the great flood of his era. He is sometimes called Xia Yu (夏禹), as it was under his rule that the first actual dynasty in China was installed, the Xia dynasty (2070 to 1600 BCE). The art and science of Feng Shui developed out of the Ho River Map and the Lo River Script, and they are still used today as the authoritative guides in determining the spatial arrangement and orientation of objects as they relate to the flow of energy (氣, qi). Interestingly, Yu is not mentioned in the *Ten Wings,* and why he was omitted is unclear.

Originally there were two distinct Before Heaven arrangements of the Eight Trigrams, one attributed to Fu Xi himself (doubtful) and the other to Yu the Great. In the one attributed to Fu Xi, the placement of the images of Valley ☱ and Mountain ☶ have been interchanged and the numbering system is different. Yu the Great's version, with Mountain and Valley in their common positions, is the one used today (see pages 38–39 for more details on the variations between these two arrangements).

King Wen (文王, Wen Wang) or Ji Chang (姬昌)

King Wen (circa 1152 BCE), also known as Ji Chang, ancestral name of Ji (姬) and his given name of Chang (昌), was never really a king, but since he is considered the founder of the Zhou dynasty, he has been given this title. King Wen's father, King Ji of Zhou, who ruled a small state along the Wei River (present Shaanxi province) had been betrayed and executed by the Shang emperor Wen Ding (文丁). Later when King Zhou of Shang (紂王), the last emperor of the Shang dynasty, feared King Wen's influence and the possibility of Wen overthrowing him, he imprisoned Wen at Youli (羑里, presently called Tangyin in Henan). It was in Youli where King Wen wrote and formed the *Book of Sun and Moon*. According to a popular tale, this is also where King Zhou, to completely subjugate King Wen, killed one of King Wen's sons and had him made into a soup, forcing King Wen to eat it.

Other officials who respected Wen bribed King Zhou with gifts of gold, jade, horses, and women, to release him. King Wen did have the intent of overthrowing King Zhou, but he died before being able to do so. His son, King Wu, however, did take rule by defeating King Zhou and started the Zhou[2] dynasty. Another of King Wen's sons, the Duke of Zhou, served as a regent for the empire and at some point earlier in his life, King Wen, and his mother it is thought, taught him the workings of the *Yi*.

King Wen married a woman by the name of Tai Si (太姒), who bore him ten sons. She was a descendant of Yu the Great, founder of the Xia dynasty. King Wen met Tai Si

---

[2] The ideogram for *Zhou* (紂) used in the title "King Zhou of Shang" is not the same ideogram as King Wu of Zhou (周).

when still a prince and walking along the Wei River where he spotted her on the other side. He was so captivated with her that he built a bridge so they could meet. This impressed her so much she agreed to marry him. It is said she was a great mother and taught all her sons the Dao of correct virtue and for attaining wisdom. In the *Book of Poetry* is a poem about a beautiful maiden gathering flowers along a river bank who is loved and adored by a prince. Legends say this poem is an account of the story of King Wen and Tai Si.

Stories say that when King Wen had to sentence criminals, he had no need to use a jail cell. He would simply place them in the courtyard, draw a circle around them, and leave them there. Criminals learned quickly it was pointless to try to escape because King Wen could simply look at the circle and see the images (trigrams and hexagrams) he needed to track them down. If a criminal escaped, King Wen would simply order his officers to the place he knew where the criminal was heading and they could just wait to arrest the escapee there. This story has some believability because the *Book of Sun and Moon* was created to develop this type of intuitive and deductive reasoning in a person.

The *Book of Sun and Moon* is a brilliant and enlightening work, and could have only been created by someone of very high wisdom and intuition. The common belief is that King Wen is the inventor of the trigram images and arrangements, both for the Before Heaven and After Heaven. He is also attributed with having created the Sixty-Four Hexagram circular and square constructs, and, obviously, for arranging the sequence of the Sixty-Four Hexagrams of the *Book of Sun and Moon* and the text explaining the Sixty-Four Hexagrams.

Duke of Zhou (周公, Zhou Gong) or Ji Dan (姬旦)

The Duke of Zhou (circa 1122 BCE), a son of King Wen, was the first Chinese official to introduce feudalism to China, claiming that the Emperor (his brother) owned everything and that everyone was his subject. The Duke of Zhou believed feudalism was the only way to save the Zhou dynasty and to unify China. The Duke of Zhou is credited with writing the explanations for each of the six lines in each hexagram —a remarkable undertaking, to say the least, which clearly shows the level of his intuition and knowledge of the *Book of Sun and Moon*.

In Confucian legends, the Duke of Zhou is the attributed author of the *Book of Poetry* (詩經, *Shi Jing*) and the *Zhou Book of Rites* (周禮姬, *Zhou Li Chi*). These attributions are, most probably, just a connection of convenience to establish the Duke of Zhou as a founding ancestor of Confucian thinking.

Confucius (公夫子, Gong Fu Zi)

Without question, Confucius (551–479 BCE), whose name means the "Great Master Gong," along with Lao Zi (老子), author of the *Scripture on the Way and Virtue,* shaped the development of Chinese culture, even into present day. Confucius was a teacher, philosopher, educator, and political figure. *Confucianism,* founded by Confucius, is a system of philosophical and ethical teachings based on the *Five Classics* (五經, *Wu Jing*). The *Book of Sun and Moon* is the first of the five Confucian classics, which include:

1. *The Book of Sun and Moon* (易經, *Yi Jing*)
2. *Classic on Poetry* (詩經, *Shi Jing*)
3. *Book of History* (尚書, *Shang Shu*)
4. *Book of Rites* (禮記, *Li Ji*)
5. *Spring and Autumn Annals* (春秋, *Chun Qiu*)

Confucius is credited with writing commentaries on the *Book of Sun and Moon,* and these are most probably the first three of the *Ten Wings:*

Prediction Commentary (彖傳, *Tuan Zhuan*)[3]
Great Symbolism Commentary (大象傳, *Da Xiang Zhuan*)[4]
Lesser Symbolism Commentary (小象傳, *Xiao Xiang Zhuan*)[5]

He may also have written the *Treatises on the Images of Qian and Kun* (文言, *Wen Yan*). The remaining seven commentaries of the *Ten Wings* are most likely compositions of his direct disciples or later Confucian scholars.

For those unfamiliar with the basics of Confucian and Daoist teachings, of which both philosophies take the *Yi* as an important work, Confucianism, in the end, is about attaining sagehood, whereas Daoism is about becoming an immortal. Equally, Confucianism promotes the ideal of biological immortality (the production of children, but mostly sons), and Daoism promotes spiritual immortality (creating an internal spirit child). The main emphasis in Confucianism is on *Benevolence* (仁, Ren), *Righteousness* (義, Yi), and *Propriety* (禮, Li)—all leading to the ideal of becoming a sage. In Daoism, it is the *Way* (道, Dao), *Virtue* (德, De), and the *"Naturally-just-so"* (自然, Zi Ran)—all leading to becoming an immortal.

---

[3] Commentary on each of the Sixty-Four Hexagrams.

[4] Commentary on the Eight Trigrams.

[5] Commentary on the lines of the hexagrams.

Despite these differences, both Confucianism and Daoism are wonderful teachings and both should be explored and studied. Some Confucian classics express Daoist ideals. *The Mean* (中用, *Zhong Yong),* in particular, reads like a Daoist work. The Song dynasty neo-Confucian Zhou Dunyi (周敦頤, 1017 to 1073 CE) created the Supreme Ultimate Symbol (太極圖, Tai Ji Tu), and both Daoism and Buddhism in China adhered to the structures of ritual ceremony according to the *Book of Rites* (禮記, *Li Ji).* The point is that there exists a very strong connection between these two ideologies despite the philosophical arguments and political differences they held against each other. Interestingly, their strongest bond seems to be with cosmology, and in particular the *Yi.* This is probably the result of Daoism being the first indigenous philosophy in China, making the *Yi* more Daoist in content. Confucianism, which developed later, adopted the *Yi* into its teachings—it did not create it.

Wang Bi (王弼)

Wang Bi (226 to 249 CE) lived during the Three Kingdoms period, serving as a minor official in the state of Cao Wei (曹魏). His two most important works were commentaries on the *Yi Jing*[6] and *Dao De Jing,* classifying him as a neo-Daoist. Wang is credited with arranging the order of the Sixty-Four Hexagrams as found in the *Modern Yi,* and also of formulating the standard method of manipulating the yarrow stalks for divination, based on the information given in the *Ten Wings* of the *Yi Jing.* This method is still in use today (see p. 123 for info on how to cast an image with yarrow stalks). Wang was a student of the Profound (or Mysterious) Studies School (玄學, Xuan Xue), which combined elements of Confucianism, Buddhism, metaphysics, mysticism, and spiritualism to render new interpretations of the *Yi Jing, Dao De Jing,* and *Zhuang Zi* (莊子).

Regarding Wang's commentaries on the *Book of Sun and Moon,* he believed that too much emphasis had been placed on the mathematics and imagery of the hexagrams by Han dynasty scholars. His approach was to look behind all this and search out a deep philosophical meaning of each hexagram. To do so he relied heavily on the philosophical principles found in the *Dao De Jing* and *Zhuang Zi.* Wang Bi died of pestilence at the age of twenty-four, but despite his short life his influence on Chinese philosophy remains strong even into present times.

---

[6] See *The Classic of Changes: A New Translation of the I Ching as Interpreted by Wang Bi.* Translated by Richard John Lynn (Columbia University Press, 2004).

Shao Yong (邵雍)

Shao Yong (1011–1077 CE) was a Song dynasty neo-Confucian, philosopher, and cosmologist, as well as a poet and historian. Despite his rank and influence, he managed to never take an official post with the government. His most influential work is a treatise on cosmogony, *The Sovereign's Ultimate Worldly Classic* (皇極經世, *Huang Ji Jing Shi*). He deeply investigated the *Book of Sun and Moon* during his life, studying alongside another famous neo-Confucian, Zhou Dunyi, creator of the Supreme Ultimate Diagram, which later became the symbol for Daoism.

From the work of Shao Yong, the companion system to *Yi Jing* divination known as the Plum Blossom Numerology of the *Book of Changes* (梅花易數, Mei Hua Yi Shu) was developed and attributed to him. This system is based on calculating the numerical values of the trigrams in conjunction with the Nine Palace charts from the older works of the Ho River Map and Lo River Script.

Shao Yong devised the systems for calculating and determining hexagrams without use of manipulating the yarrow stalks. The first system, called the Before Heaven Formula, looks at the situation and time when asking a question to determine the upper and lower trigrams. The second system, called the After Heaven Formula, made use of the numbering patterns and associations found in the Lo River Script to determine a hexagram for interpretation.[7]

Another of his great contributions to the *Book of Sun and Moon* was the formation of the Before Heaven Eight Houses chart of the Sixty-Four Hexagrams. Shao Yong was a student of the Image and Numerological Studies of the *Book of Sun and Moon,* as opposed to the Principles of Righteousness Studies maintained by the Confucian fundamentalists. Men like Shao Yong, his colleague Zhou Dunyi, and many others, classified as neo-Confucians, were in many ways more Daoist than Confucianist in their interests and works.

---

[7] For more information on these two remarkable systems of calculating images, see *I Ching Numerology* by Da Liu (Harper & Row Publishers, 1979).

Zhou Dunyi (周敦頤)

Zhou Dunyi (1017–1073 CE) was a neo-Confucianist philosopher and cosmologist who created the Supreme Ultimate Diagram and the term "the Illimitable" (無極, Wu Ji). His two popular works are *Explanations of the Supreme Ultimate Diagram* (太極圖說, *Tai Ji Tu Shuo*)[8] and *The Book of All-Knowing* (通書, *Tong Shu*), a reinterpretation of the *Book of Sun and Moon* still used today by many Feng Shui masters and destiny diviners.

The works of Zhou Dunyi are focused on forming a unity between Confucian ethics and Daoist naturalism, and in defining the relationships between human nature and conduct with the more celestial concepts of cosmic forces, for which the goal for human beings is to master their vital-energy (氣, qi) and so return to nature (Daoist naturalism).

His writings contained much on the theories of Wu Ji, Tai Ji, Yin and Yang, and the Five Elements, all of which are still in use today. If not for Zhou Dunyi and his colleague Shao Yong, the *Book of Sun and Moon* could have withered away into obscurity, but their works breathed new life into the theories and functions of the *Book of Sun and Moon*.

Zhou Dunyi's Depiction of Wuji Becoming Taiji

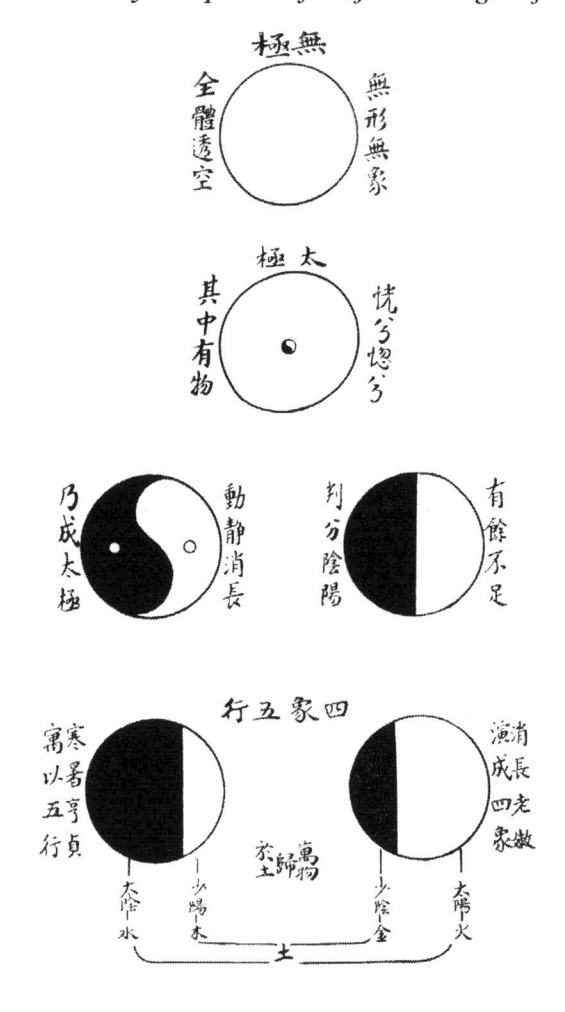

---

8   See *T'ai Chi According to the I Ching: Embodying the Principles of the Book of Changes* by Stuart Alve Olson for a full translation of this text (Inner Traditions, 2001). Zhou Dunyi's illustration of Wuji Becoming Taiji is from *Tai Ji Quan Illustrated and Explained* (太極拳圖說, *Tai Ji Quan Tu Shuo*) by Chen Pinsan, edited by Chen Panling.

Daoist Alchemical and Cosmology Masters

Wei Boyang (魏伯陽)

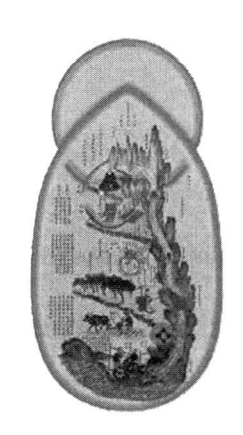

Wei Boyang lived sometime during the later years of the Han dynasty (206 BCE to 220 CE). Around 140 CE, he wrote *The Triple Unity of the Three in Accordance to the Book of Zhou* (周易參同契, *Zhou Yi Cantong Qi*).[9] Wei was an internal alchemist and is considered the first patriarch of the Southern Sect of Perfect Realization (全真南派, Quan Zhen Nan Pai). Wei wrote the *Zhou Yi Cantong Qi* using the *Book of Sun and Moon,* as well as a great deal of terminology from the *Yellow Court Scripture* (黃庭經, *Huang Ting Jing),* as models for describing the processes of creating the internal elixir for immortality. *The Triple Unity of the Three in Accordance to the Book of Zhou* melds three systems of teaching and self-cultivation—the *Book of Sun and Moon*, Daoist Non-Action (無為, Wu Wei), and Internal Alchemy (內丹, Nei Dan)—into one doctrine. His insights into the *Book of Sun and Moon* are some of the most profound in Chinese literature. Curiously, Wei was also the first Chinese person to write out the formula and process for making gunpowder.

Zhang Boduan (張伯端)

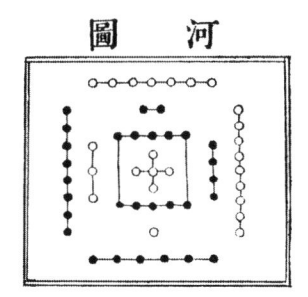

Zhang Boduan (987?–1082 CE) was a Song dynasty scholar of the Three Teachings (Confucianism, Daoism, and Buddhism) who turned to internal alchemy and Chan Buddhism in the later years of his life. He was posthumously appointed as the Second Patriarch of the Southern Sect of Perfect Realization.

---

[9] See *The Seal of the Unity of the Three: A Study and Translation of the Cantong Qi, the Source of the Taoist Way of the Golden Elixir* by Fabrizio Pregadio (Golden Elixir Press, 2011) for a complete translation of this work.

Zhang wrote two important books on internal alchemy: *Tablets on Understanding Reality* (悟真篇, *Wu Zhen Pian*)[10] and the *Four Hundred Words on the Golden Elixir* (金丹四百字, *Jin Dan Si Bai Zi*). Both works make a strong connection with the *Book of Sun and Moon*. In his *Four Hundred Words on the Golden Elixir*, Zhang prefaces the work with the Ho River Map.

Liu Yiming (劉一明)

Liu Yiming (1734–1821 CE) was an eleventh generation Daoist master of the Dragon Gate Sect (龍悶派, Long Men Pai). He wrote numerous commentaries on Daoism, specifically on internal alchemy. The *Book of Sun and Moon* plays a significant role in his explanations of Daoist theories and philosophy. He wrote several books on it—the main one being *Revealing the Truth of the Zhou Book of Changes* (周易闡真, *Zhou Yi Zhan Zhen*). Liu's works provide some of the best commentaries on Daoism. Even though he advocated and wrote on the Three Teachings of Daoism, Confucianism, and Buddhism, his overriding themes focused on Daoism and the correlations of the *Book of Sun and Moon*.

---

[10] See *Understanding Reality* by Chang Po-tuan, with commentary by Liu I-ming. Translated by Thomas Cleary (University of Hawaii Press, 1987).

Part Two

History of the Book of Sun and Moon

The Three *Yi* Books

A statement in *The Rituals of the Zhou Dynasty* (周禮, *Zhou Li*) says,

> The Great Diviner was in charge of the three *Yi*: *Connecting Mountains Yi*, *Returning to the Treasure-House Yi,* and the *Zhou Dynasty Book of Changes*.[11]

From this record, we know there were originally three different *Yi* books, but only the *Zhou Yi* survived the book burning in the Qin dynasty by the tyrant emperor Qin Shi Huang Di (秦始皇帝—246 to 221 BCE). The big question here is whether the other two *Yi* books were the model for the present *Yi*, or vice versa? Since neither of the other two books are extant this question remains unanswered.

Another question is, "Did King Wen use or know of the two missing *Yi* books?" Since it is stated in *The Rituals of the Zhou Dynasty* that during the time of the Zhou dynasty three separate *Yi* books existed, and since the family of King Wen's wife, Tai Si, were descendants of Yu the Great, it is highly probable that King Wen had access to these two missing works. What import they had on his forming the present *Book of Sun and Moon* will remain a mystery unless they are unearthed in the future.

The *Original Yi* and *Modern Yi*

In this section, the *Book of Sun and Moon* will be referred to in its simpler form, as the *Yi*. The *Original Yi* (本易, *Ben Yi*) consists of the *Sixty-Four Hexagrams* (卦, *Gua*), the *Prediction* (彖, *Tuan*)[12] by King Wen, and the *Explanation of the Individual Lines* (爻, *Yao*) by the Duke of Zhou. Together, these three parts comprise the original framework of the *Yi*, or as it is called the *Original Yi* (see *Book of Sun and Moon,* volume II).

Some four hundred years after the *Original Yi* was written by King Wen and Duke of Zhou, Confucius wrote his commentaries on the *Great* and *Lesser Symbolism* and on King

---

[11] *Great Diviner* (大卜, Da Bu). The *Three Yi* are *Connecting Mountains Yi* (連山易, *Lian Shan Yi*), *Returning to the Treasure-House Yi* (歸藏易, *Gui Zang Yi*), and the *Zhou Dynasty Book of Changes* (周易, *Zhou Yi*). This statement on the *Three Yi* comes from *I Ching Book of Changes* by Ch'u Chai.

[12] The *Prediction* (彖, *Tuan*) comprises King Wen's explanations of the Sixty-Four Hexagrams.

Wen's *Prediction*. Later, seven additional commentaries were compiled, most likely written by disciples of Confucius, as in many cases they state, "The Master said …" making it unlikely Confucius wrote them. In the end, these works collectively became known as the *Ten Wings*.

The *Modern Yi* (今易, *Jin Yi*) was compiled by Fei Zhi (費直) in the first Han dynasty (206 BCE to 220 CE). In the *Modern Yi*, the first five wings of the *Ten Wings* act as commentaries on the three main parts of the *Original Yi*. Before the *Modern Yi*, the *Ten Wings* were a completely separate book from the *Original Yi*.

Ten Wings (十翼, Shi Yi)[13]

First Wing:	*The Image* (彖傳, *Tuan Zhuan*).
	Commentary on King Wen's *Tuan (Prediction)* of each hexagram.
Second Wing:	*The Great Symbolism* (大象傳, *Da Xiang Zhuan*).
	Commentary on the trigrams of an image.
Third Wing:	*The Lesser Symbolism* (小象傳, *Xiao Xiang Zhuan*).
	Commentary on each line in the hexagrams.
Fourth Wing:	*The Wen Yan* (文言) *on Qian* (乾).
	Commentary on the hexagram Qian ䷀.
Fifth Wing:	*The Wen Yan* (文言) *on Kun* (坤).
	Commentary on the hexagram Kun ䷁.
Sixth Wing:	*The Upper Appendix* (繫辭上傳, *Xi Ci Shang Zhuan*).
	Twelve sections, primarily describing the functions of the hexagrams.
Seventh Wing:	*The Lower Appendix* (繫辭下傳, *Xi Ci Xia Zhuan*).
	Twelve sections, primarily discussing the meaning of the trigrams.
Eighth Wing:	*Treatise of Remarks on the Trigrams* (說卦傳, *Shuo Gua Zhuan*).
	Eleven sections discussing the correlations of the trigrams and the use of the stalks.
Ninth Wing:	*The Orderly Sequence of the Images* (序卦傳, *Xu Gua Zhuan*).
	Two sections giving a description on the ordering of the hexagrams in a manner showing their natural progression of events.

---

[13] Note: Originally the second and third wings were one wing, but the first book was *Great Symbolism and Lesser Symbolism* (of the first thirty images) combined into one wing. The lower book was also divided so that the *Great Symbolism* and *Lesser Symbolism* occurred for the remaining thirty-four images. These then were counted as two wings and the *Wen Yan* as one wing. For easier clarification, I have made the *Wen Yan* into two separate wings and do not divide the *Great Symbolism* and *Lesser Symbolism* into two separate wings.

Tenth Wing: *The Blending of the Hexagrams Treatise* (雜卦傳, *Za Gua Zhuan*). A brief description explaining the oppositions and complementary correspondences of the hexagrams.

Arrangement of Hexagrams from the Tenth Wing

The Blending of the Hexagrams Treatise (雜卦傳, *Za Gua Zhuan*) in the Tenth Wing presents the following order of the Sixty-Four Hexagrams. This sequence may very well be the original ordering of the Sixty-Four Hexagrams by King Wen. Wang Bi is said to have reorganized them into the sequence we see today. The numbers above each hexagram correspond to Wang Bi's positioning of the images, shown in their proper numerical order in the following section. Including the numbers here helps show how this original arrangement differs from Wang Bi's and gives further evidence that Wang changed the ordering of the hexagrams for some reason.

#1	#2	#8	#7	#19	#20	#3	#4
#51	#52	#41	#42	#26	#25	#45	#46
#15	#16	#21	#22	#57	#58	#17	#18
#23	#24	#35	#36	#48	#47	#31	#32
#59	#60	#40	#39	#38	#37	#12	#11
#34	#33	#14	#13	#49	#50	#62	#61
#55	#56	#30	#29	#9	#10	#5	#6
#28	#44	#53	#27	#63	#54	#64	#43

Upper and *Lower Books* of the *Yi*

The *Yi* is divided into two separate books. Hexagrams #1 thru #30 constitute the *Upper* (or first) *Book,* and hexagrams #31 thru #64 make up the *Lower* (second) *Book.*

The first book begins with the hexagrams of #1 *Creativity of Heaven* (the Heaven trigram ☰ doubled ䷀) and #2 *Receptivity of Earth* (the Earth trigram ☷ doubled ䷁). It ends with #29 *The Abyss* (the Water trigram ☵ doubled ䷜) and #30 *Distant Brightness* (the Fire trigram ☲ doubled ䷝). These Four Cardinal Hexagrams—representing South (Heaven ☰), North (Earth ☷), East (Fire ☲), and West (Water ☵)—as seen in the Before Heaven Arrangement of the Eight Trigrams, are the framing/foundational images of the first book.

The Four Cardinal Hexagrams in the *Upper Book* are:

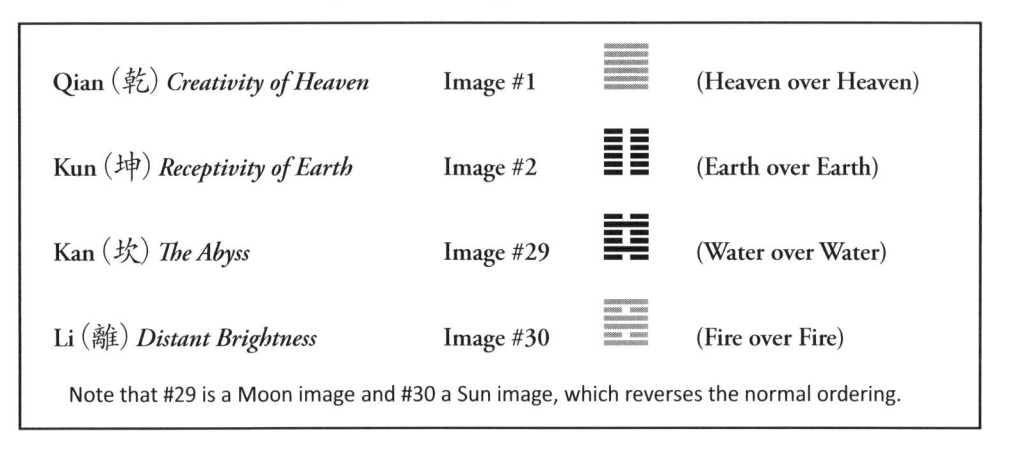

Qian (乾) *Creativity of Heaven*	Image #1	䷀	(Heaven over Heaven)
Kun (坤) *Receptivity of Earth*	Image #2	䷁	(Earth over Earth)
Kan (坎) *The Abyss*	Image #29	䷜	(Water over Water)
Li (離) *Distant Brightness*	Image #30	䷝	(Fire over Fire)

Note that #29 is a Moon image and #30 a Sun image, which reverses the normal ordering.

Eclipse Images: Hexagrams #27 *Nourishment* (頤, Yi) and #28 *Great Passing* (大過, Da Guo) represent eclipses of the Sun and Moon. *Nourishment,* #27, represents the Moon eclipsing the Sun, and *Great Passing,* #28, represents the Sun eclipsing the Earth. These images are also in reverse order, as #28 is a Sun image and #27 a Moon image.

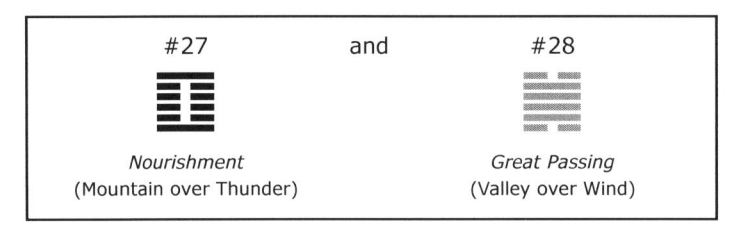

#27	and	#28
䷚		䷛
Nourishment (Mountain over Thunder)		Great Passing (Valley over Wind)

The second book begins with #31 *Attraction* ䷞ (Valley ☱ over Mountain ☶) and #32 *Constancy* ䷟ (Thunder ☳ over Wind ☴), and ends with the hexagrams of #63 *After Completion* ䷾ (Water ☵ over Fire ☲) and #64 *Before Completion* ䷿ (Fire ☲ over Water ☵). It is important to note here that the first book begins with the images that represent Heaven and Earth, and ends with Water and Fire, the images of the Moon and Sun. The second book begins with the hexagrams of Valley over Mountain and Thunder over Wind, which represent the four diagonal directions—Southeast (Valley ☱), Northeast (Thunder ☳), Southwest (Wind ☴), and Northwest (Mountain ☶), and ends with the images of Fire and Water (Sun and Moon) intermixed with each other.

Unlike the *Upper Book*, wherein the doubled images are positioned at the beginning and end of the sequence of hexagrams, the doubled hexagrams in the *Lower Book* are positioned internally of the other hexagrams. Although the theories on the ordering of the hexagram images will be touched upon later, and fully explained in a future work, suffice to say the division of the *Upper* and *Lower Books* is extremely important to both the interpretation and construction of the *Yi*.

The four doubled hexagrams in the *Lower Book* are:

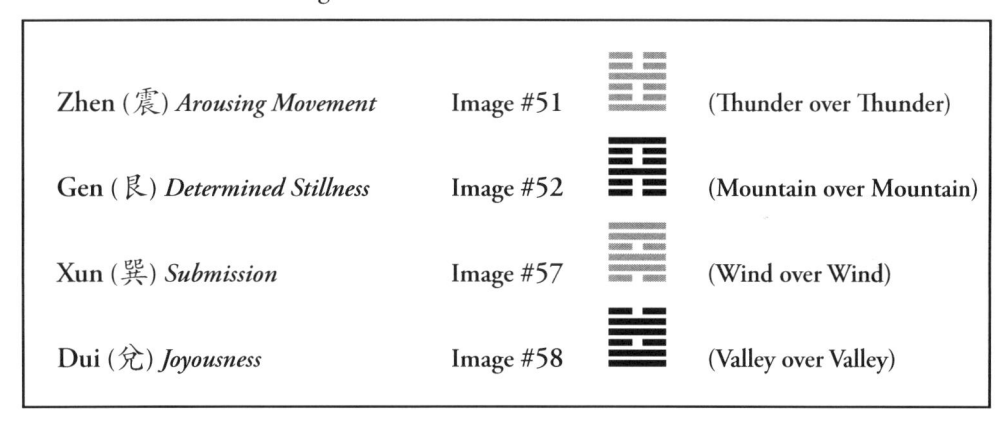

Zhen (震) *Arousing Movement*	Image #51	䷲	(Thunder over Thunder)
Gen (艮) *Determined Stillness*	Image #52	䷳	(Mountain over Mountain)
Xun (巽) *Submission*	Image #57	䷸	(Wind over Wind)
Dui (兌) *Joyousness*	Image #58	䷹	(Valley over Valley)

Eclipse Images: Hexagrams #61 *Inner Truth* (中孚, Zhong Fu) and #62 *Small Passing* (小過, Xiao Guo) represent partial, or half, eclipses of the Sun and Moon. Image #61 represents the Moon eclipsing the Sun, and #62 the Sun eclipsing the Earth.

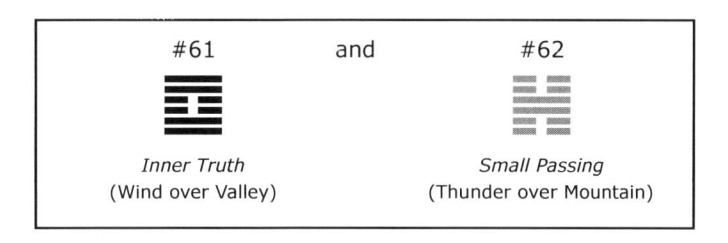

#61	and	#62
䷼		䷽
Inner Truth (Wind over Valley)		*Small Passing* (Thunder over Mountain)

Book of Sun and Moon

Diagram of Hexagrams in the *Upper Book* (Images #1 thru #30)

The four doubled hexagrams of the *Upper Book*—#1, #2, #29, and #30—correlate to the four solar periods, four cardinal directions, and four celestial animals.

Heaven (South) is symbolized by the *Red Bird* (Summer Solstice)

Earth (North) is symbolized by the *Black Turtle* (Winter Solstice)

Water (West) is symbolized by the *Green Dragon* (Spring Equinox)

Fire (East) is symbolized by the *White Tiger* (Autumn Equinox)

Diagram of Hexagrams in the *Lower Book* (Images #31 thru #64)

#31	#32	#33	#34	#35	#36
#37	#38	#39	#40	#41	#42
#43	#44	#45	#46	#47	#48
#49	#50	#51	#52	#53	#54
#55	#56	#57	#58	#59	#60
		#61	#62		
		#63	#64		

The four doubled hexagrams of the *Lower Book*—#51, #52, #57, and #58—correlate to the four seasons, four diagonal directions, and four celestial animals.

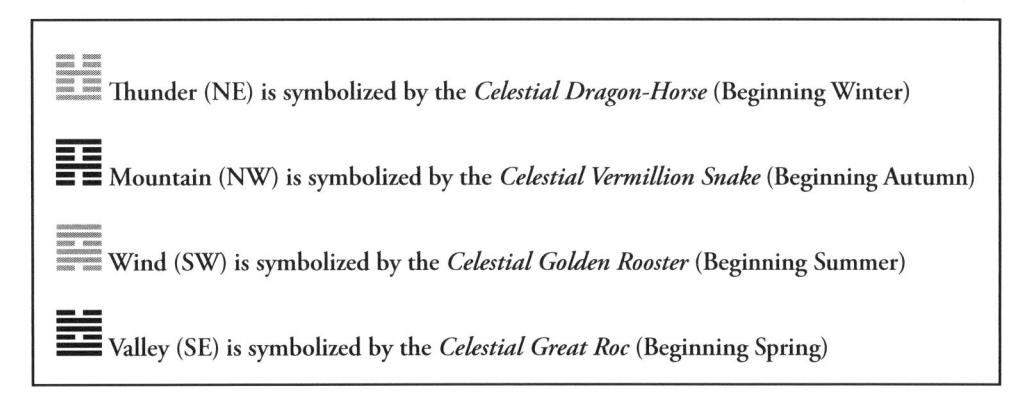

Thunder (NE) is symbolized by the *Celestial Dragon-Horse* (Beginning Winter)

Mountain (NW) is symbolized by the *Celestial Vermillion Snake* (Beginning Autumn)

Wind (SW) is symbolized by the *Celestial Golden Rooster* (Beginning Summer)

Valley (SE) is symbolized by the *Celestial Great Roc* (Beginning Spring)

An interesting change in the pattern of images occurs with hexagrams #29 and #30, and #63 and #64 (as well as the Eclipse images). In #29 *The Abyss* and #30 *Distant Brightness,* for example, the Sun and Moon ordering is reversed. Hexagram #29 is a Moon/Yin image, and #30 is a Sun/Yang image. Images #1 thru #26 all follow the Sun and Moon, or Yang and Yin, pattern with odd-numbered hexagrams being Yang, and even-numbered images as Yin. Yet at the very end of the *Upper Book,* the pattern is reversed. The same is true for the hexagrams at the end of the second book. *After Completion,* #63, is a Moon/Yin hexagram, and *Before Completion,* #64, is a Sun/Yang hexagram. The question, then, is why reverse the proper placement of these hexagrams at the ends of each book?

The answer is most likely found in how Wang Bi constructed the order of the hexagrams in each book. The quick explanation is that in examining the *Upper Book* we find thirty hexagrams that correlate with the Nine Palaces numbering system of fifteen (see p. 70). The *Upper Book* begins with hexagram #1 ䷀ (Heaven over Heaven) and #2 ䷁ (Earth over Earth). It ends with hexagram #29 ䷜ (Water over Water), and #30 ䷝ (Fire over Fire). So the first book makes a full cycle and interchange of Heaven and Earth, and Water and Fire, and the entire first book is based on these Four Pillar (or cardinal) hexagrams of Heaven, Earth, Water, and Fire. In the *Upper Book,* these four cardinal hexagrams appear on the four external positions with the remaining twenty-six images appearing and contained within them. As will be detailed in *The Logic of the Formation of the Sixty-Four Hexagrams,* this interchange is the basis for determining the sequential order of the hexagrams in the *Lower Book.*

The *Lower Book* is based on the Nine Palaces numbering system of the older (Fu Xi) trigram arrangement wherein the number eighteen is the sum number, and is based on the four doubled diagonal hexagrams of Valley, Mountain, Thunder, and Wind. These four hexagrams appear within the remaining thirty hexagrams surrounding them, an opposite positioning as seen in the first book.

Regarding hexagrams #63 and #64, the last two hexagrams of the *Lower Book,* which also reverse their Sun and Moon positioning, they are formed on the trigrams of Water ☵ and Fire ☲. Fire is the After Heaven trigram of Heaven ☰, and Water is the After Heaven trigram of Earth ☷, and so this shows a return to the original position shown in King Wen's placement of the After Heaven trigrams around the Before Heaven trigrams.

In *The Philosophy of Fortune-Telling of the Eight Character Horoscopes* (八字推命哲學, *Ba Zi Tui Ming Zhe Xue),* it is said,

> Therefore, the images of the Before Heaven and After Heaven trigrams, the After Heaven encircles the Before Heaven to create the images. Just like the Moon moving around the Earth. So when the Sun comes, the Moon departs; when the Moon arrives, the Sun leaves.
> 故先天圖而後天圖之卦,生卦為後天轉圈先天.
> 如一月旋地. 日來月出, 月來日出.
> Gu Xian Tian Tu Er Hou Tian Tu Zhi Gua, Sheng Gua Wei Hou Tian Zhuan Quan Xian Tian. Ru Yi Yue Xuan Di. Ri Lai Yue Chu, Yue Lai Ri Chu.

In *A Collection on the Essentials of the Rivers He and Luo,* it states,

> Before Heaven images are fixed; the After Heaven images become movable.
> 先天卦是定,後天卦為動.
> Xian Tian Gua Shi Ding, Hou Tian Gua Wei Dong.

From this statement it can be deduced that the After Heaven trigrams (outer circle of trigrams in the graphic to the right), being a temporal condition, are in constant motion. The Before Heaven (inner circle of trigrams), being primordial, are therefore fixed in position. So by placing the After Heaven trigrams around the Before Heaven ones, there is then the opportunity of moving the After Heaven images around the Before Heaven trigrams in a precise manner to create the various Sixty-Four Hexagrams, and this may very well be what King Wen and Wang Bi had done to determine their ordering of the Sixty-Four Hexagram arrangements.

When examining the thirty hexagrams of the *Upper Book,* there are fifteen Sun/Yang images and fifteen Moon/Yin images. If the *Lower Book* includes the hexagrams of #29 and #30, by reversing them into their proper positions and counts them with the remaining thirty-four images, the total number of hexagrams in the *Lower Book* would be thirty-six. This means that dividing the *Lower Book* into an equal number of Sun/Yang and Moon/Yin images, the total of each would be eighteen.

By having eighteen Sun hexagrams and eighteen Moon hexagrams, the order and numbering of the hexagrams for the *Lower Book* can be correlated with the original Before Heaven Arrangement of the Eight Trigrams attributed to Fu Xi, wherein the central number is six and all surrounding numbers equal eighteen (see section of the Nine Palaces starting on p. 69). The number eighteen is also important in that it takes eighteen changes to create a six-lined image when using the stalks. Meaning, for the creation of one line of a hexagram there are three sorting stages of the stalks. All six lines, then, take eighteen total sorting actions.

Also note that the first two hexagrams of the *Lower Book,* #31 ䷞ and #32 ䷟, are a combination of all four diagonal trigrams in the Before Heaven Arrangement (Valley ☱ and Mountain ☶, Thunder ☳ and Wind ☴). These four are also the main doubled trigrams (#58 ䷹, #52 ䷳, #51 ䷲, #57 ䷸) of the *Lower Book.*

29

These theories on the Before Heaven and After Heaven arrangements and how they may have influenced the ordering of the Sixty-Four Hexagrams may seem confusing at this point in the book, but after some careful study of the entire work, the framing and structure of the *Book of Sun and Moon* will prove logical. Basically, how King Wen and Wang Bi may have constructed and placed the Sixty-Four Hexagrams (briefly hinted at here, but fully detailed in a future work) are based on two simple formulas: 1) the numbering used when manipulating the fifty stalks, and 2) the manner of how the After Heaven Arrangement of the Eight Trigrams is moved and circled around the Before Heaven Arrangement.

Neither of these theories should be of any great surprise to *Book of Sun and Moon* enthusiasts as the method of manipulating stalks was presented by the ancient sages for good reason and purpose. Their use forms a very integrated and fundamental function in the *Book of Sun and Moon*.

Part Three

Formation of the Trigrams and Hexagrams

The entire *Book of Sun and Moon* is premised and constructed on the two symbolic lines of *Yin* and *Yang* (陰陽)—with the solid line representing Yang, and the broken line Yin. These are called the *Two Powers* (兩儀, Liang Xiang).

Yang   Yin

From these two lines, the Yin and Yang are stacked upon each other to create, with the proper concordance of moving the Yin and Yang lines, the *Four Images* (四像, Si Xiang). Notice that the upper line alternates Yang, Yin, Yang, Yin, and the lower line moves Yang, Yang, Yin, Yin.

Heaven   Sun   Moon   Earth
Sky   Fire   Water   Soil

From these Four Images the influences of the *Three Powers* (三才, San Cai) are introduced, thus making the *Eight Trigrams* (八卦, Ba Gua) consisting of three lines each.

| 1 | 2 | 3 | 4 | 5 | 6 | 7 | 8 |
| Heaven | Valley | Fire | Thunder | Wind | Water | Mountain | Earth |

Notice that the Four Images from above appear as the top two lines of each trigram and are repeated to make eight.

Also, starting in position 1 and moving across the bottom lines of each trigram to the right, there is a movement of four Yang lines and then four Yin lines. The second line moves across in pairs of Yang Yang, Yin Yin, Yang Yang, and Yin Yin symbols. The third, upper, line then uses the alternating pattern of Yang and Yin symbols.

Tai Ji Creation of the Two Powers, Four Emblems, and Eight Trigrams[14]

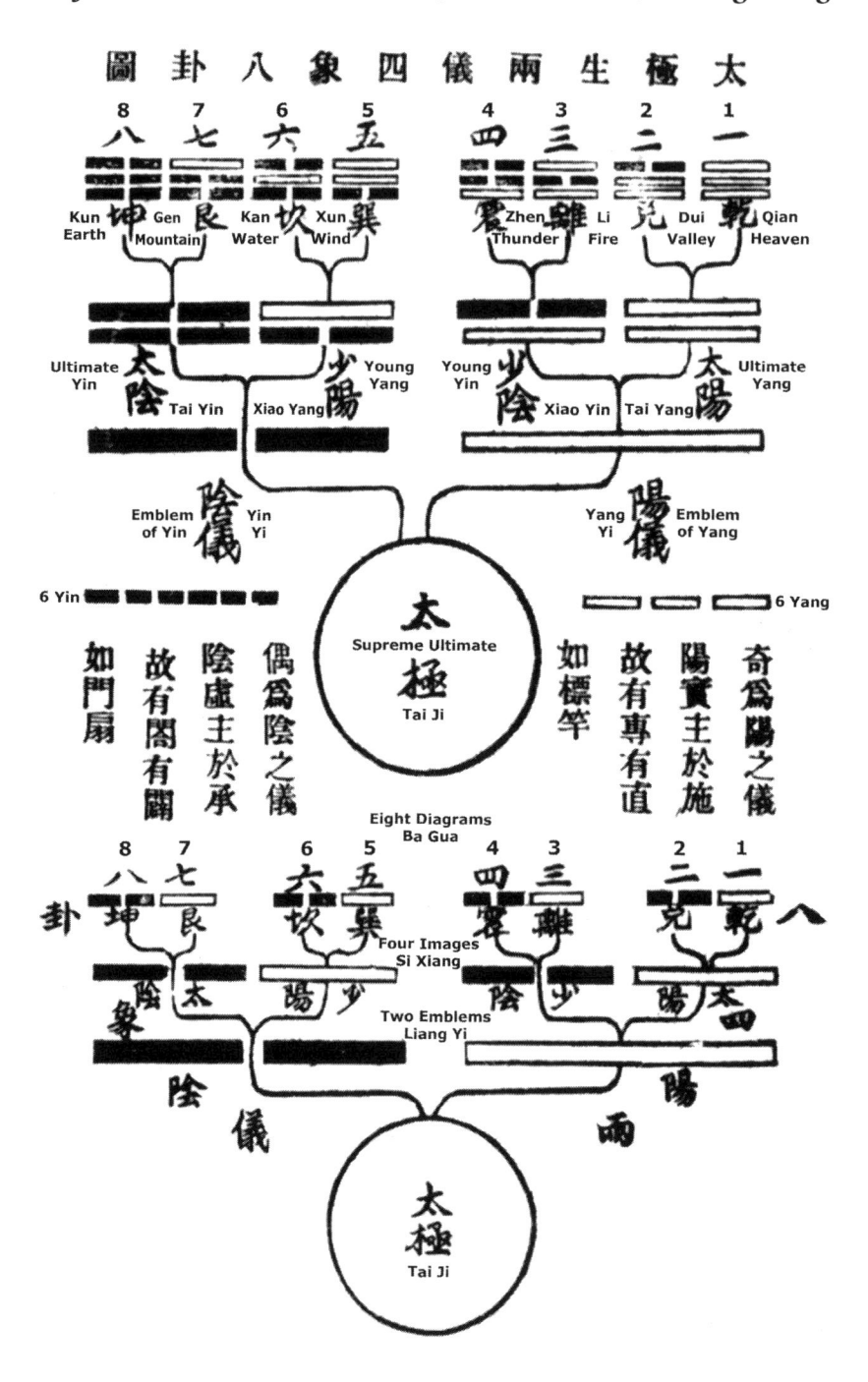

---

[14] This diagram shows the development of the Yin and Yang lines to complete the Eight Trigrams. From *Tai Ji Quan Illustrated and Explained* (太極拳圖說, *Tai Ji Quan Tu Shuo*) by Chen Pinsan, edited by Chen Panling.

Text (Center Right Side)

The emblem of Yang is eminent.	奇為陽之儀	
	Qi Wei Yang Zhi Yi	
The ruler of the substantial is exhibited in the Yang.	陽實主於施	
	Yang Shi Zhu Yu Shi	
Hence, it has purpose and straightness,	故有專有直	
	Gu You Zhuan You Zhi	
like a signal post.	如標竿	
	Ru Biao Gan	

Text (Center Left Side)

The emblem of Yin is mating.	偶為陰之儀	
	Ou Wei Yin Zhi Yi	
The ruler of the insubstantial is contained in the Yin.	陰虛主於承	
	Yin Xu Zhu Yu Cheng	
Hence, it has entrances and openings,	故有闔有闢	
	Gu You Ge You Pi	
just like the leafs of a door.	如門扇.	
	Ru Men Shan.	

From the creation of the Eight Trigrams they were then put in a circular arrangement, usually placed around the Supreme Ultimate Symbol (太極圖, Tai Ji Tu). The movement of the trigrams follow the same pattern as in the linear arrangement. However, in the circular arrangement, the trigrams do not travel around the circle in a clockwise or counterclockwise fashion, but instead they follow the curve and motion of the Supreme Ultimate Symbol—starting at the top with Heaven, moving down to Valley, then to Fire, and Thunder before crossing over to Wind, down to Water, then to Mountain, and lastly to Earth.

Before Heaven Arrangement

Another way of looking at this arrangement of trigrams is by looking at the assignments given to each of them:

	Sun/Yang Trigrams			**Moon/Yin Trigrams**	
	☰ Heaven / Sky / Father / S			☷ Earth / Soil / Mother / N	
☱ Valley / Morning / SE / Youngest Daughter	☲ Fire / Sun / E / Middle Daughter	☳ Thunder / Afternoon / NE / Eldest Son	☴ Wind / Evening / SW / Eldest Daughter	☵ Water / Moon / W / Middle Son	☶ Mountain / Night / NW / Youngest Son

The Three Powers in the Trigrams and Hexagrams

In chapter 2 of *Treatise of Remarks on the Trigrams,* the following verse clearly establishes the use of the Three Powers within the trigrams and hexagrams:

> Anciently, when the sages constructed the *Yi,* they brought forth and followed the principles of Nature and Life. Thus they established the Dao of Heaven, calling it Yin and Yang; the Dao of Earth, calling it the yielding and unyielding; and the Dao of Humanity, calling it benevolence and righteousness. Therefore, they united the Three Powers with the two. Hence, the six lines of the images were completed. Separating the Yin and separating the Yang repeatedly, the six positions of the images were completed.
>
> 昔者聖人之作易也.將以順性命之理.是以立天之道.
> 曰陰與陽.立地之道.曰柔與剛.立人之道.曰仁與義.兼三
> 才而兩之.故易六畫而成卦.分陰分陽.迭用柔剛.故易六
> 位而成章.
>
> Xi Zhe Sheng Ren Zhi Zuo Yi Ye. Jiang Yi Shun Xing Ming Zhi Li. Shi Yi Li Tian Zhi Dao. Yue Yin Yu Yang. Li Di Zhi Dao. Yue Rou Yu Gang. Li Ren Zhi Dao. Yue Ren Yu. Jian San Cai Er Liang Zhi. Gu Yi Liu Hua Er Cheng Gua. Fen Yin Fen Yang. Die Yong Rou Gang. Gu Yi Liu Wei Er Cheng Zhang.

In a trigram, the first (bottom) line represents Earth, the second (middle) line represents Humanity, and the third (top) line represents Heaven. In a hexagram (six-lined image) the bottom two lines represent Earth, the two middle lines represent Humanity, and the two top lines represent Heaven.

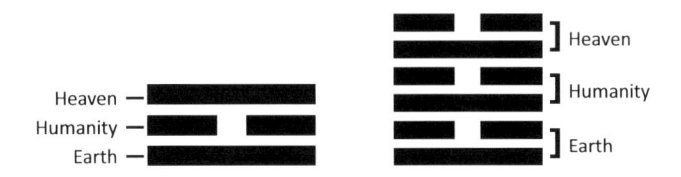

One of the ideas expressed in the Three Powers is that Humanity (人, Ren) sits between Heaven and Earth. In Huang Di's *Yin Convergence Scripture,* it states,

> When Heaven manifests its destructive powers, the stars move and the constellations shift. When Earth manifests its destructive powers, dragons and serpents rise to dry land. When Humanity manifests its destructive powers, Heaven and Earth are overturned.
>
> 天發殺機,移星易宿,地發殺機,龍蛇起陸,
> 人發殺機,天地反覆.
>
> Tian Fa Sha Ji, Yi Xing Yi Su, Di Fa Sha Ji, Long She Qi Lu, Ren Fa Sha Ji, Tian Di Fan Fu.

This verse is stating that Humanity is the most powerful of the Three Powers, and upon Humanity relies even the existence of Heaven and Earth. In the *Yi*'s images—trigrams and hexagrams—the middle line or middle two lines represent Humanity. This is also seen in the creation of the Inner Image of a hexagram, wherein the second, third, and fourth lines make up the lower trigram of the Inner Image, and the third, fourth, and fifth lines create the upper trigram. In both cases, the third and fourth lines are used—the middle two lines that represent Humanity.

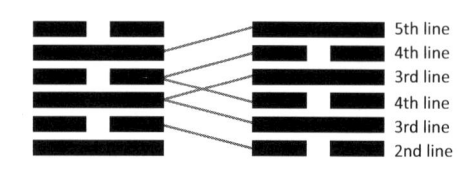

Three Powers Era Cycles

The influences of the Three Powers are also used within the calculation of eras.

    Every 180 years constitutes a Small Era (three cycles of sixty years)—Earth.

    Every 1,080 years constitutes a Common Era (six cycles of 180 years)—Humanity.

    Every 9,720 years constitutes a Great Era (nine cycles of 1,080 years)—Heaven.

Present Three Powers Small-Era Cycle:

    1864 to 1923 (Upper, Heavenly, Period)

    1924 to 1983 (Middle, Humanly, Period)

    1984 to 2043 (Lower, Earthly, Period)

Part Four

The Eight Trigram Arrangements

In chapter 11 of the *Upper Appendix* (繫辭上傳, *Xi Ci Shang Zhuan*) it says,

> In the two divisions *[Upper* and *Lower Books* of the *Yi]* the calculated number for all possible variations is 11,250. This number corresponds to the Ten Thousand Things.

而篇之策, 萬有一千五百二十. 當萬物之數也.

Er Pian Zhi Ce, Wan You Yi Qian Wu Bai Er Shi. Dang Wan Wu Zhi Shu Ye.

From these Sixty-Four Hexagrams and the possible changing lines that could occur when casting a hexagram, we arrive at 11,520 variations, or as it is collectively called, the Ten Thousand Things (萬物, Wan Wu). This term *Wan Wu* is normally presented simply as the auspicious emblem 卍 (pronounced Wan).

One way of determining this calculation is based on mathematically examining the manipulation of the stalks. Hence, to generate all Sixty-Four Hexagrams, there must be two divisions of the stalks (into a Sun pile and a Moon pile) for each casting. Taking one stalk and then sorting by fours from the piles gives the number five, which must be done three times to get one line, which means the number three is multiplied six times (the number of lines in a hexagram). Mathematically speaking, then, 2 x 5 x 3 x 6 x 64 (the total number of hexagrams) equals 11,520.

The simplest way to derive this number is to multiply one hexagram, times the Ten Heavenly Stems (十翼), which are the five Yin and five Yang possibilities of any given line, times eighteen changes (since it takes three sorting changes of the stalks to make one line of a hexagram, creating six lines takes eighteen), times sixty-four (total number of hexagrams), and this will arrive at 11,520 (1 x 10 x 18 x 64 = 11,520).[15]

---

[15] Another way of arriving at this number is to take any given hexagram and then go through the process of changing one line, then determine all the possibilities of changing two lines, then all the possibilities of three lines, then all the possibilities of four lines, then all the possibilities of five lines, and then six, and the final number will be 11,520.

Original Before Heaven Arrangement

The first and older version of arranging the Eight Trigrams, attributed to Fu Xi, shows the positions of Mountain and Valley reversed from the following version by Yu the Great. In chapter 3 of the *Treatise of Remarks on the Trigrams,* it says,

> Heaven and Earth have fixed positions, but the influences of Mountains and Marshes [Valleys] are interchangeable.
> 天地定位, 山澤通氣.
> Tian Di Ding Wei, Shan Ze Tong Qi.

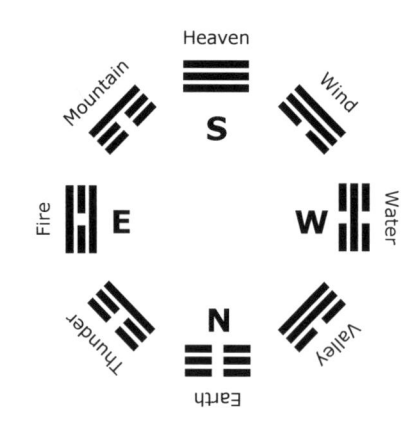

It may be that this original configuration of the Eight Trigrams was arranged this way to make the assignments on the left side more Yang and the right side more Yin. In Yu the Great's (newer) Before Heaven Arrangement, the family assignments of Valley and Youngest Daughter are placed in the Southeast, and Mountain and Youngest Son are placed in the Northwest. Fu Xi's arrangement allows for three males to be on the Yang side and three females on the Yin side, thus having Yin (Fire ☲) within the Yang, and Yang (Water ☵) within the Yin, just as the Supreme Ultimate Diagram shows.

Even though this particular arrangement is not pertinent to the use of divination and calculation as shown in the *Book of Sun and Moon*, it is relevant to the structure of the *Lower Book* of the *Yi*, which will be explained in the companion work *The Logic of the Formation of the Sixty-Four Hexagrams.*

Older Linear Version of the Before Heaven Arrangement

1	2	3	4	5	6	7	8
☰	☶	☲	☳	☴	☵	☱	☷
Heaven	Mountain	Fire	Thunder	Wind	Water	Valley	Earth

Family and Gender Assignments of the Older Before Heaven Arrangement of the Eight Trigrams

Three male figures and one female are represented on the Yang/East side of the arrangement:

☰   Heaven (Qian) is the Father or commanding male leader.

☶   Mountain (Gen) is the Youngest Son or a young male.

☲ Fire (Li) is the Middle Daughter or a middle-aged female.

☳ Thunder (Zhen) is the Eldest Son or an older male.

Three female figures and one male are represented on the Yin/West side of the arrangement:

☴ Wind (Xun) is the Eldest Daughter or an older female.

☵ Water (Kan) is the Middle Son or a middle-aged male.

☱ Valley (Dui) is the Youngest Daughter or a young female.

☷ Earth (Kun) is the Mother or an empowered female leader.

Newer Before Heaven Arrangement

This standard arrangement, attributed to Yu the Great, represents the primordial influences and constructs of Nature through eight emblems. The idea of Before Heaven (先天, Xian Tian) indicates the conditions of Nature before Humanity even existed. For example, Heaven is the sky, and Earth is everything beneath the sky. Heaven creates everything (萬物, Wan Wu, the Ten Thousand Things) and Earth receives and nourishes all of creation. Valleys and Mountains create and complement each other. All things flow down (like water) into Valleys, the low places of Earth, and all things ascend to Mountains (such as water evaporating and then returning to rain). Fire and Water create and complement each other. These two can be thought of as the Sun and Moon, light and darkness, heating and cooling, dryness and moistening, and so on. Thunder and Wind create and complement each other. Thunder (lightning, earthquakes, sound) causes movement and so Wind is created, and Wind moves the clouds, spreads seeds, and conditions the climate. So from these eight primordial influences and constructs all of Nature is created and perpetuated.

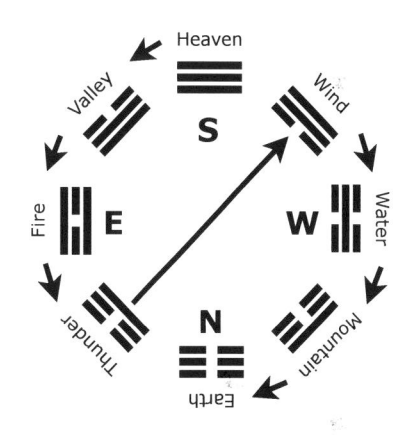

The movement of the trigrams of the Before Heaven start in the South (☰ Heaven) and end in the North (☷ Earth), with the intermediary or crossover trigrams running from the Northeast (☳ Thunder) to the Southwest (☴ Wind).

Newer Linear Version of the Before Heaven Arrangement

1	2	3	4	5	6	7	8
☰	☱	☲	☳	☴	☵	☶	☷
Heaven	Valley	Fire	Thunder	Wind	Water	Mountain	Earth

Family and Gender Assignments of the Newer Before Heaven Arrangement of the Eight Trigrams

Two male figures and two females are represented on the Yang/East side of the arrangement:

☰ Heaven (Qian) is the Father or commanding male leader.

☱ Valley (Dui) is the Youngest Daughter or young girl.

☲ Fire (Li) is the Middle Daughter or middle-aged female.

☳ Thunder (Zhen) is the Eldest Son or an older male.

Two female figures and two males are represented on the Yin/West side of the arrangement:

☴ Wind (Xun) is the Eldest Daughter or an older female.

☵ Water (Kan) is the Middle Son or a middle-aged male.

☶ Mountain (Gen) is the Youngest Son or a young male.

☷ Earth (Kun) is the Mother or an empowered female leader.

Contrasted Image Arrangement

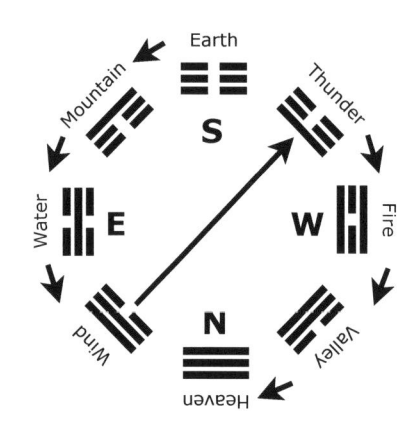

The Contrasted Images are not only the direct opposite of the Before Heaven trigrams, they are the actual power of the Before Heaven images. For example, without Earth there can be no Heaven, without Mountains there can be no Valleys, without Water there can be no Fire, and without Wind there can be no Thunder. These Eight Contrasted Image Trigrams act like the opposite sides of a coin. There are always two sides to any influence or condition. This arrangement reveals the duality of everything—*Yin-Yang, male-female, light-dark,* and so on—and the dependence that dual relationships have on one another. In essence, Earth depends not just on Heaven but on Mountains and Valleys, Water and Fire, and Wind and Thunder in which to continually perpetuate and nourish itself. Just as Heaven does not solely depend on Earth, it needs Valleys and Mountains, Fire and Water, and Thunder and Wind in which to continually create.

The movement of the trigrams of the Contrasted Image arrangement starts in the North (☷ Earth) and finishes in the South (☰ Heaven), with the intermediary or crossover images running Northeast (Wind ☴) to Southwest (Thunder ☳).

Linear Version of the Contrasted Image Arrangement

1	2	3	4	5	6	7	8
☷	☶	☵	☴	☳	☲	☱	☰
Earth	Mountain	Water	Wind	Thunder	Fire	Valley	Heaven

Family and Gender Assignments of the Contrasted Image Arrangement of the Eight Trigrams

Two male figures and two females are represented on the Yang/East side of the arrangement.

- ☷ Earth (Kun) is the Mother or empowered female leader.
- ☶ Mountain (Gen) is the Youngest Son or young male.
- ☵ Water (Kan) is the Middle Son or middle-aged male.
- ☴ Wind (Xun) is the Eldest Daughter or older female.

Two female figures and two males are represented on the Yin/West side of the arrangement.

- ☳ Thunder (Zhen) is the Eldest Son or an older male.
- ☲ Fire (Li) is the Middle Daughter or a middle-aged female.
- ☱ Valley (Dui) is the Youngest Daughter or a young girl.
- ☰ Heaven (Qian) is the Father or commanding male leader.

Eight Gates Arrangement

This arrangement of trigrams, attributed to Shao Yong, is like the link between the Before Heaven and After Heaven images. This arrangement signifies gates opening and leading the Before Heaven and Contrasted trigrams to the After Heaven trigrams. The movement of the trigrams of the Eight Gates functions in the same manner as those of the After Heaven, starting in the North (☲ Fire) and ending in the South (☵ Water), with the intermediary or crossover images running from the Southwest (☶ Mountain) to the Northeast (☷ Earth).

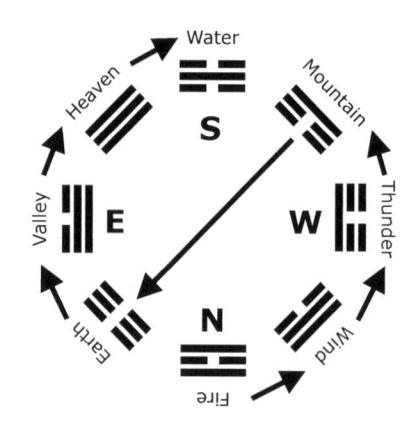

The Eight Gates trigrams are determined as the After Heaven trigrams of the Contrasted images. For example, if the hexagram *Adversity* (#12, Heaven over Earth ䷋) was cast, the Opposite/Contrasted hexagram would be *Peacefulness* (#11, Earth over Heaven ䷊). The After Heaven trigram of Earth (☷) is Water (☵) and the After Heaven trigram of Heaven (☰) is Fire (☲), so the Eight Gates hexagram would be Water over Fire ䷾ (image #63, *After Completion*).

Linear Version of the Eight Gates Arrangement

8	7	6	5	4	3	2	1
☵	☰	☱	☷	☶	☳	☴	☲
Water	Heaven	Valley	Earth	Mountain	Thunder	Wind	Fire

Family and Gender Assignments of the Eight Gates Arrangement of the Eight Trigrams

Two female figures and two males are represented on the Yin/West side of the arrangement.

☲   Fire (Li) is the Middle Daughter or a middle-aged female.

☴   Wind (Xun) is the Eldest Daughter or an older female.

☳   Thunder (Zhen) is the Eldest Son or an older male.

☶   Mountain (Gen) is the Youngest Son or a young male.

Two male figures and two females are represented on the Yang/East side of the arrangement.

⚏ Earth (Kun) is the Mother or the empowered female.

☱ Valley (Dui) is the Youngest Daughter or a young female.

☰ Heaven (Qian) is the Father or a commanding male leader.

☵ Water (Kan) is the Middle Son or a middle-aged male.

After Heaven Arrangement

The After Heaven Arrangement of the Eight Trigrams, attributed to King Wen, and its connection to the Before Heaven Arrangement of images must be examined. Although the primary reason may be linked to the formation and ordering of the Sixty-Four Hexagrams, it is also true that the After Heaven trigrams correlate with the Before Heaven images to show both the primordial conditions and temporal functions of life.

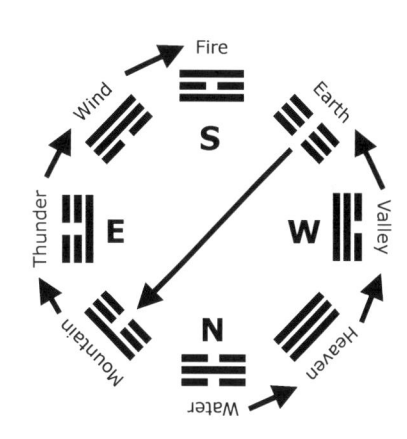

This arrangement represents the temporal influences and constructs of Nature through eight emblems. The idea of After Heaven (後天, Hou Tian) indicates the conditions of Nature after Humanity came into existence. The movement of the trigrams of the After Heaven starts in the North (☵ Water) and ends in the South (☲ Fire), with the intermediary or crossover images running from the Southwest (⚏ Earth) to the Northeast (☶ Mountain).

The meaning of the After Heaven arrangements is one of the least discussed and most misunderstood aspects of the *Book of Sun and Moon*. One manner of looking at why King Wen arranged the trigrams the way he did can be determined by the function of the After Heaven (AH) trigrams to the Before Heaven (BH) trigrams. For example:

☰ Heaven (BH) is visible due to the brightness of ☲ Fire (AH).

Heaven (or sky) can be seen by humanity because of Fire (light from the Sun, Moon, and stars). Fire is then the clarity of Heaven.

⛰ Valleys (BH) are nourished by ☴ Wind (AH).

Valleys (oceans, rivers, streams, lakes, marshes) are formed and made useful to humanity through Wind (descending movements of gravity and magnetic attraction). Everything flows down into the low places.

☲ Fire (BH) is the expression of ☳ Thunder (AH).

Fire (heat, light, breath) is created by Thunder (the spark of life). Humanity comes into existence because of Thunder, the very inception of life. Thunder, as lightning, is also a bright flash of nitrogen cleansing the air of negative ions, as well as making all plants greener and, in turn, enabling them to produce more oxygen.

☳ Thunder (BH) produces ☶ Mountains (AH).

Thunder (an earthquake) creates Mountains (ascending movements and magnetic repulsion). Thunder causes things to burst forth and ascend, everything from a seed bursting forth to the Big Bang theory of our very cosmos.

☴ Wind (BH) moves and forms the ☷ Earth (AH).

Wind (gravitational pull) affects the Earth (the planet). Wind also regulates the climate of the Earth, shifting clouds and creating high and low pressure areas.

☵ Water (BH) flows and collects into ☱ Valleys (AH).

Water consumes and enters all low places, Valleys. Water is the most yielding yet strongest of all elements. Nothing defeats Water because it fills all the hollows and empty spaces. Water nourishes the Valleys so Humanity can grow food.

☶ Mountains (BH) are ☰ Heaven (AH) on Earth.

Mountains are ascending and function as Heaven on Earth. Mountains produce precious metals and so enrich Humanity with valuable gold, silver, and so on, thus bringing material prosperity to people, just as Heaven invests Humanity with spiritual riches. Mountains are places of enlightenment where the Heavenly Mind is discovered.

☷ Earth (BH) is revealed by ☵ Water (AH).

The planet Earth is four-fifths water, just as is the human body. When Water is on the Earth, life flourishes and the seasons can be determined.

The After Heaven Creation Trigrams (Mountain, Thunder, Wind, and Fire)
☶ ☳ ☴ ☲

Mountains and Thunder are the creators of the movement (Wind) of Fire (the Sun).

On the left side of the After Heaven Arrangement it can be seen that Mountains create Thunder (such as the shaking sounds of earthquakes). Thunder then creates Wind, producing movement, and from Wind, Fire is then nourished (fires feed off oxygen).

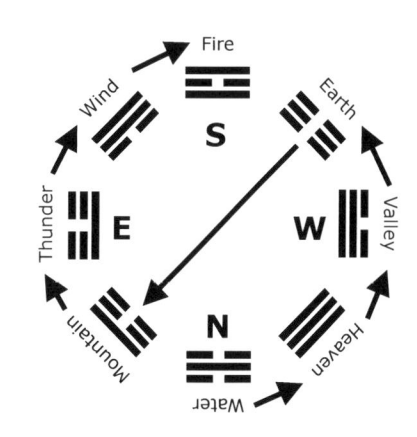

In looking at these images in reverse it can be seen that Fire (heat) creates Wind (movement). From movement (Wind) there is a bursting forth (Thunder), and Thunder ascends to create Mountains.

In nature we can see all this as the progression, for example, of a volcano: heat (lava, Fire) is moved (Wind) wherein the movement builds to an eruption (Thunder) through the top of a Mountain. It can also be seen in the development of a plant: the seed seeking the light of the Sun (germination, Fire) moves (mutation, Wind) to burst through the soil (Thunder) and grows upward as a plant (Mountain).

The After Heaven Nourishing Trigrams (Water, Heaven, Valley, and Earth)
☵ ☰ ☱ ☷

Waters coming down from the sky (Heaven), collecting in the Valleys to nourish the Earth.

On the right side, the image movements show Water (evaporation) rising into the sky (atmosphere, Heaven) where rain then falls from the sky into the Valleys and so nourishes the Earth. In reverse, the images show that from within the Earth, Valleys (oceans, rivers, marshes) are created. From these places, water evaporates into the sky (Heaven), where rain (Water) is then produced.

In nature, the progression of these images can be seen as the Water (semen) of the male (Heaven) is collected (Valley) in the female (Earth). Or, in reverse, the female (Earth) receives (Valley) the male (Heaven) semen (Water). Or, Water from the sky (Heaven) gathers in (the Valley) and nourishes the soil (Earth).

The following image shows the connection and relationships of these trigrams according to the After Heaven Arrangement.[16] Wind, for example, moves through Heaven (the sky), dispersing the clouds. Thunder (lightning, sparks) create Fire. Earth creates and supports Mountains. Water flows into the Valleys, creating rivers, lakes, and oceans.

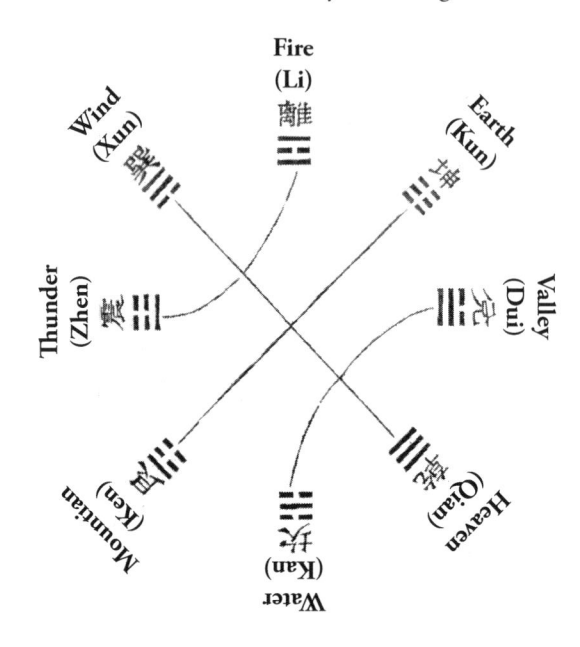

Linear Version of the After Heaven Arrangement

8	7	6	5	4	3	2	1
Fire	Wind	Thunder	Mountain	Earth	Valley	Heaven	Water

Family and Gender Assignments of the After Heaven Arrangement of the Eight Trigrams

Two female figures and two males are represented on the Yin/West side of the arrangement.

- Water (Kan) is the Middle Son or a middle-aged male.
- Heaven (Qian) is the Father or a commanding male leader.
- Valley (Dui) is the Youngest Daughter or a young female.
- Earth (Kun) is the Mother or an empowered female leader.

---

[16] From *A Collection on the Essentials of the Rivers He and Luo* (河洛精蘊, *He Luo Jing Yun*).

Two male figures and two females are represented on the Yang/East side of the arrangement.

- ☶ Mountain (Gen) is the Youngest Son or a young male.
- ☳ Thunder (Zhen) is the Eldest Son or an older male.
- ☴ Wind (Xun) is the Eldest Daughter or an older female.
- ☲ Fire (Li) is the Middle Daughter or middle-aged female.

The Four Linear Arrangements of the Eight Trigrams

Before Heaven Arrangement

1	2	3	4	5	6	7	8
Heaven	Valley	Fire	Thunder	Wind	Water	Mountain	Earth

Contrasted Image Arrangement

1	2	3	4	5	6	7	8
Earth	Mountain	Water	Wind	Thunder	Fire	Valley	Heaven

Eight Gates Arrangement

8	7	6	5	4	3	2	1
Water	Heaven	Valley	Earth	Mountain	Thunder	Wind	Fire

After Heaven Arrangement

8	7	6	5	4	3	2	1
Fire	Wind	Thunder	Mountain	Earth	Valley	Heaven	Water

The Four Circular Arrangements of the Eight Trigrams

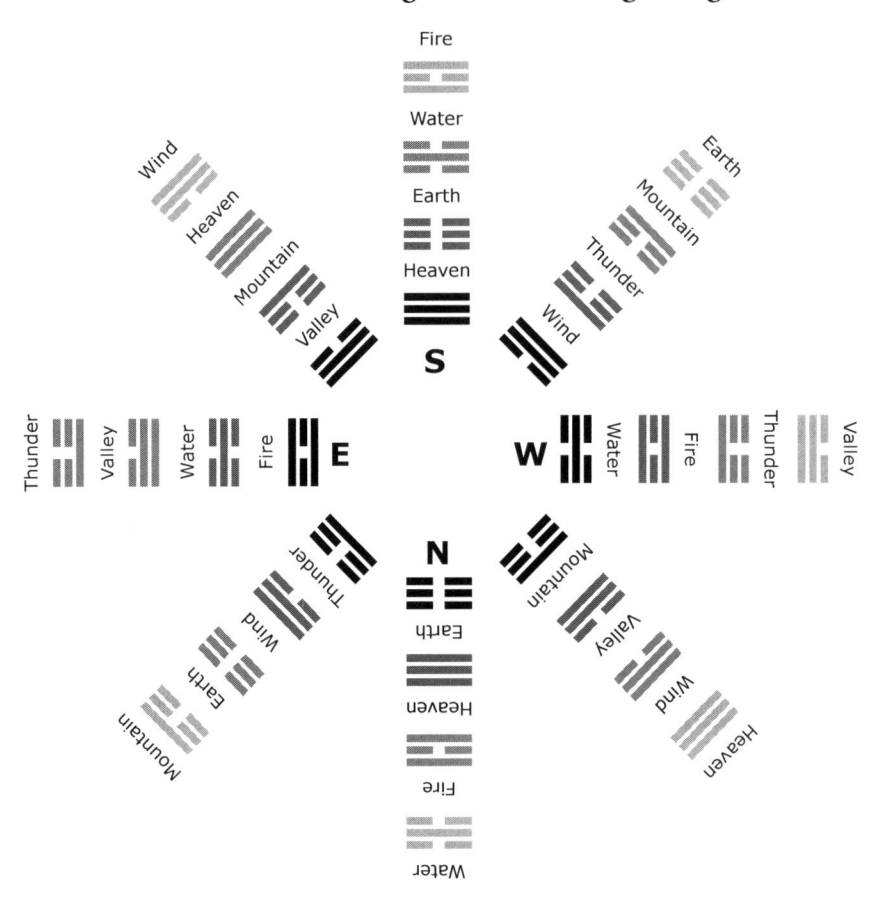

▬▬▬ Before Heaven Arrangement [first, innermost circle]

≡ ≡ Contrasted Image Arrangement [second circle]

≡ ≡ Eight Gates Arrangement [third circle]

▬▬▬ After Heaven Arrangement [fourth circle]

Part Five

The Eight Houses of the Sixty-Four Hexagrams

In the previous section, four main arrangements of the Eight Trigrams were shown. Now, by stacking the trigrams on top of each other, the Sixty-Four Hexagrams can be revealed and likewise grouped into the same four types of arrangements:

1) Before Heaven Sixty-Four Hexagram Arrangement.
2) Contrasted Image Sixty-Four Hexagram Arrangement.
3) Eight Gates Sixty-Four Hexagram Arrangement.
4) After Heaven Sixty-Four Hexagram Arrangement.

These four arrangements of hexagrams are distinctly different from the ordering of the Sixty-Four Hexagrams in the *Original* and the *Modern Yi* (see *Book of Sun and Moon*, volume II) as well as from the hexagram arrangements of the Sixty-Year Cycle (see p. 76). In the following four arrangements, the Sixty-Four Hexagrams are grouped into eight houses of eight-related hexagrams, which are then, like the Eight Trigram arrangements, presented in linear-square and circular representations.

The Eight Houses of the Before Heaven Arrangement of Hexagrams

Shao Yong arranged the Sixty-Four Hexagrams into eight sections, or Eight Houses (八房, Ba Fang), with each house containing the hexagrams that define that house. The *House of Heaven*, for example, contains the eight hexagrams that have Heaven (☰) as the lower trigram. The order of the upper trigrams change according to the sequence of the Before Heaven Arrangement of the Eight Trigrams. For example:

1st ☰ House of Heaven, Qian 乾

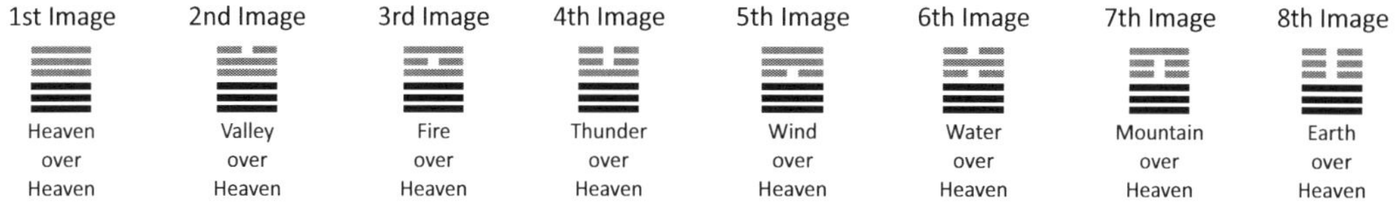

1st Image	2nd Image	3rd Image	4th Image	5th Image	6th Image	7th Image	8th Image
Heaven over Heaven	Valley over Heaven	Fire over Heaven	Thunder over Heaven	Wind over Heaven	Water over Heaven	Mountain over Heaven	Earth over Heaven

Linear-Square Arrangement of the Eight Houses of the Before Heaven Hexagrams

1st ☰ House of Heaven, Qian 乾

#1	#43	#14	#34	#9	#5	#26	#11
Creativity of Heaven	Decision	Great Possession	Great Strength	Small Accumulation	Hesitation	Great Accumulation	Peacefulness

2nd ☱ House of Valley, Dui 兑

#10	#58	#38	#54	#61	#60	#41	#19
Treading	Joyousness	Opposition	Marriageable Maiden	Inner Truth	Regulating	Sacrifice	Approaching

3rd ☲ House of Fire, Li 離

#13	#49	#30	#55	#37	#63	#22	#36
People United	Revolution	Distant Brightness	Prosperity	The Family	After Completion	Adornment	Diminishing Light

4th ☳ House of Thunder, Zhen 震

#25	#17	#21	#51	#42	#3	#27	#24
Innocence	Following	Mastication	Arousing Movement	Increase	Beginning Difficulties	Nourishment	Returning

5th ☴ House of Wind, Xun 巽

#44	#28	#50	#32	#57	#48	#18	#46
Pairing	Great Passing	The Cauldron	Constancy	Submission	The Well	Inner Destruction	Ascending

6th ☵ House of Water, Kan 坎

#6	#47	#64	#40	#59	#29	#4	#7
Contending	Oppression	Before Completion	Liberation	Dispersion	The Abyss	Untaught Youth	The Army

7th ☶ House of Mountain, Gen 艮

#33	#31	#56	#62	#53	#39	#52	#15
Retreating	Attraction	The Wanderer	Small Passing	Gradual Movement	Difficult Obstruction	Determined Stillness	Modesty

8th ☷ House of Earth, Kun 坤

#12	#45	#35	#16	#20	#8	#23	#2
Adversity	Collecting	Advancement	Joyful Ease	Contemplation	Union	Removing	Receptivity of Earth

The Eight Houses of the Sixty-Four Hexagrams

Circular Arrangement of the Before Heaven Eight Houses

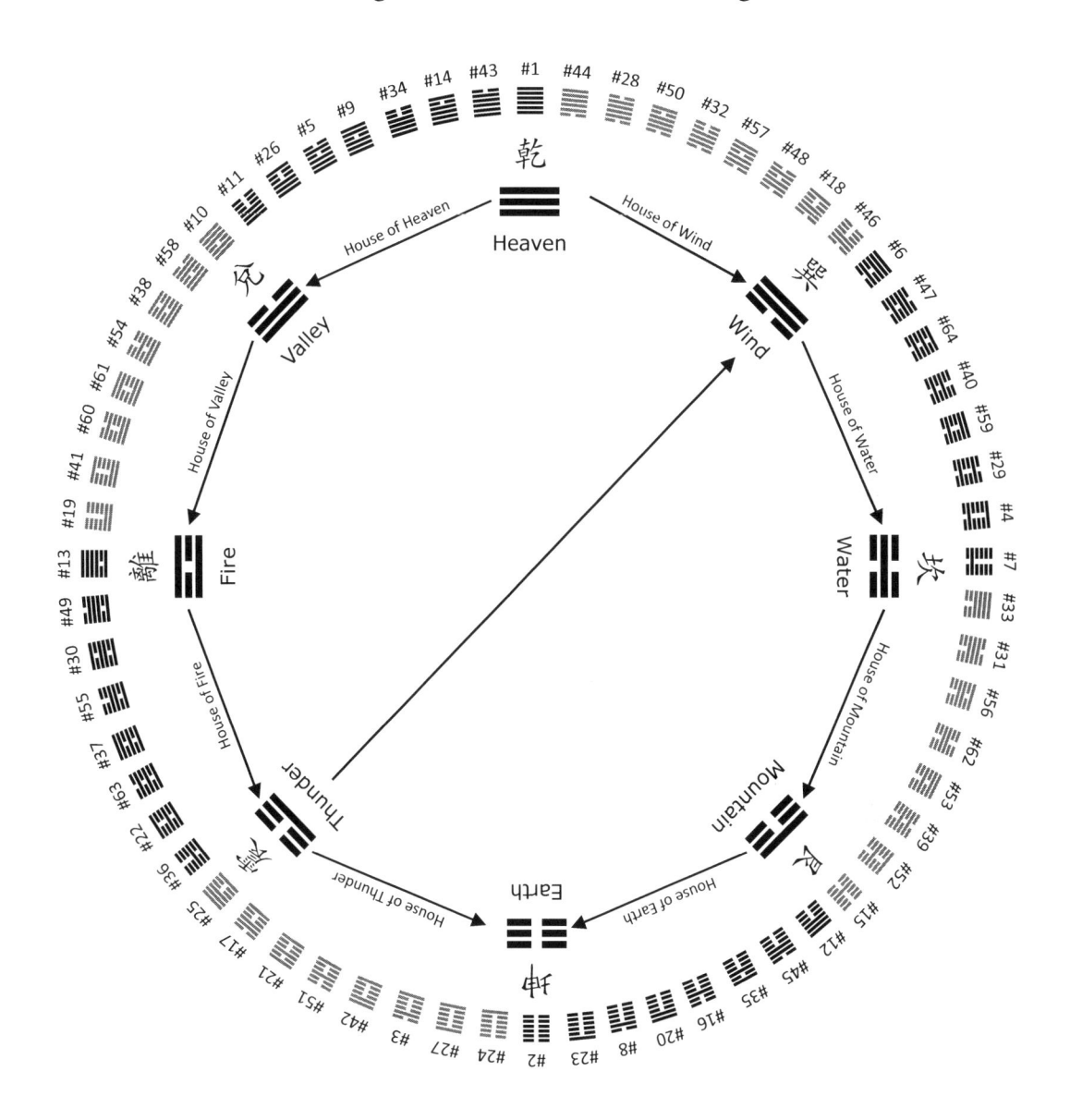

The Eight Houses of the Contrasted Image Arrangement of Hexagrams

These hexagrams follow the same pattern of movement as in the Before Heaven circular arrangement, but each hexagram position is exactly opposite. The Contrasted Images are formed by rotating the circular Before Heaven graphic 180 degrees so that #2 *Receptivity of Earth* appears at the top, rather than #1 *Creativity of Heaven*.

Circular Arrangement of the Contrasted Image Eight Houses

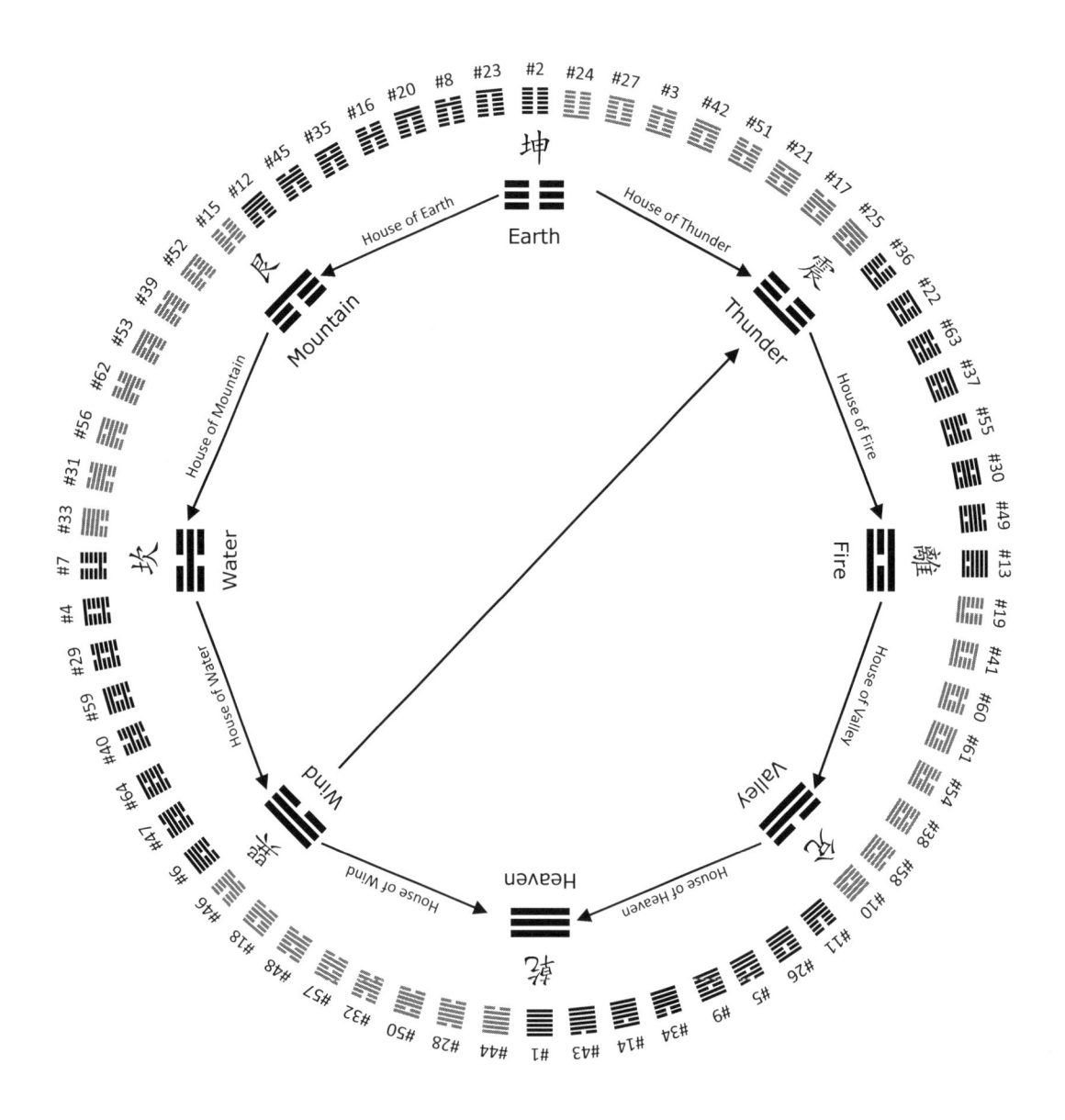

Linear-Square Arrangement of the Eight Houses of the Contrasted Image Hexagrams

1st ☷ House of Earth, Kun 坤

#2	#23	#8	#20	#16	#35	#45	#12
Receptivity of Earth	Removing	Union	Contemplation	Joyful Ease	Advancement	Collecting	Adversity

2nd ☶ House of Mountain, Gen 艮

#15	#52	#39	#53	#62	#56	#31	#33
Modesty	Determined Stillness	Difficult Obstruction	Gradual Movement	Small Passing	The Wanderer	Attraction	Retreating

3rd ☵ House of Water, Kan 坎

#7	#4	#29	#59	#40	#64	#47	#6
The Army	Untaught Youth	The Abyss	Dispersion	Liberation	Before Completion	Oppression	Contending

4th ☴ House of Wind, Xun 巽

#46	#18	#48	#57	#32	#50	#28	#44
Pairing	Great Passing	The Cauldron	Constancy	Submission	The Well	Inner Destruction	Ascending

5th ☳ House of Thunder, Zhen 震

#24	#27	#3	#42	#51	#21	#17	#25
Returning	Nourishment	Beginning Difficulties	Increase	Arousing Movement	Mastication	Following	Innocence

6th ☲ House of Fire, Li 離

#36	#22	#63	#37	#55	#30	#49	#13
Diminishing Light	Adornment	After Completion	The Family	Prosperity	Distant Brightness	Revolution	People United

7th ☱ House of Valley, Dui 兌

#19	#41	#60	#61	#54	#38	#58	#10
Approaching	Sacrifice	Regulating	Inner Truth	Marriageable Maiden	Opposition	Joyousness	Treading

8th ☰ House of Heaven, Qian 乾

#11	#26	#5	#9	#34	#14	#43	#1
Peacefulness	Great Accumulation	Hesitation	Small Accumulation	Great Strength	Great Possession	Decision	Creativity of Heaven

The Eight Houses of the Eight Gates Arrangement of Hexagrams

The Eight Houses of the Eight Gates are derived by linking the After Heaven Houses to their corresponding houses in the Contrasted Image arrangement.

The Eight Gates Houses follow a pattern of changing lines to move through the eight hexagrams of each house. The *House of Kun,* for example, begins with image #2 *Receptivity of Earth,* which is the image of Earth ☷ doubled ䷁. The other houses start with their respective doubled images as well, with Fire over Fire for the *House of Fire,* Water over Water for the *House of Water,* and so on.

The pattern of changing lines can be seen clearly, for example, by looking at the *House of Kun:*

5th ☷ House of Earth, Kun 坤

Trigram Movement from Earth to Heaven

1st Image	2nd Image	3rd Image	4th Image	5th Image	6th Image	7th Image	8th Image
Earth Doubled	1st line changed	2nd line changed	3rd line changed	4th line changed	5th line changed	4th line changed	1st–3rd lines changed

Note how the upper trigram of Earth (☷) moves across the top of the hexagrams (in the After Heaven position) until reaching the fourth hexagram/image, where it then changes to its opposite (Heaven ☰) in the Before Heaven (lower trigram) position. This Heaven trigram then moves across four positions until Earth (☷) returns as the lower trigram in the eighth hexagram. This identical pattern of trigram movement occurs in all Eight Houses.

Each house also follows the same pattern of changing lines that occurs in the second through seventh images, with the complete change of the lower trigram back to its original starting trigram in the eighth image/position.

Linear-Square Arrangement of the Eight Gates Eight Houses

8th ☵ House of Water, Kan 坎 (Trigram Movement from Water to Fire)

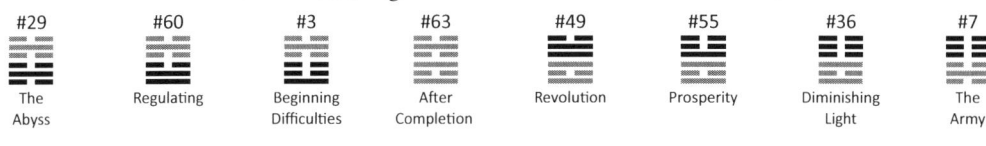

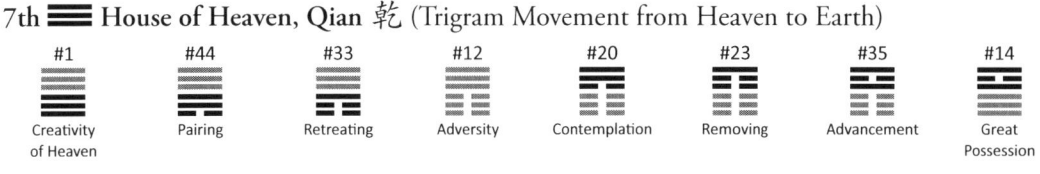

#29	#60	#3	#63	#49	#55	#36	#7
The Abyss	Regulating	Beginning Difficulties	After Completion	Revolution	Prosperity	Diminishing Light	The Army

7th ☰ House of Heaven, Qian 乾 (Trigram Movement from Heaven to Earth)

#1	#44	#33	#12	#20	#23	#35	#14
Creativity of Heaven	Pairing	Retreating	Adversity	Contemplation	Removing	Advancement	Great Possession

6th ☱ House of Valley, Dui 兌 (Trigram Movement from Valley to Mountain)

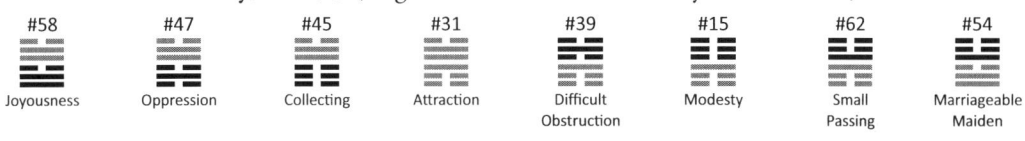

#58	#47	#45	#31	#39	#15	#62	#54
Joyousness	Oppression	Collecting	Attraction	Difficult Obstruction	Modesty	Small Passing	Marriageable Maiden

5th ☷ House of Earth, Kun 坤 (Trigram Movement from Earth to Heaven)

#2	#24	#19	#11	#34	#43	#5	#8
Receptivity of Earth	Returning	Approaching	Peacefulness	Great Strength	Decision	Hesitation	Union

4th ☶ House of Mountain, Gen 艮 (Trigram Movement from Mountain to Valley)

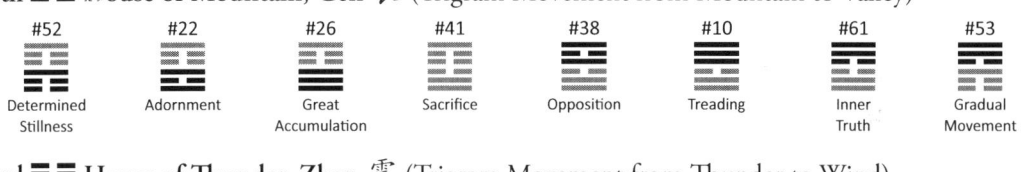

#52	#22	#26	#41	#38	#10	#61	#53
Determined Stillness	Adornment	Great Accumulation	Sacrifice	Opposition	Treading	Inner Truth	Gradual Movement

3rd ☳ House of Thunder, Zhen 震 (Trigram Movement from Thunder to Wind)

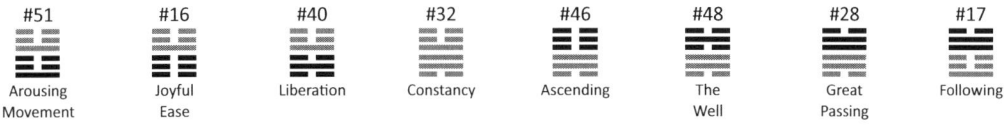

#51	#16	#40	#32	#46	#48	#28	#17
Arousing Movement	Joyful Ease	Liberation	Constancy	Ascending	The Well	Great Passing	Following

2nd ☴ House of Wind, Xun 巽 (Trigram Movement from Wind to Thunder)

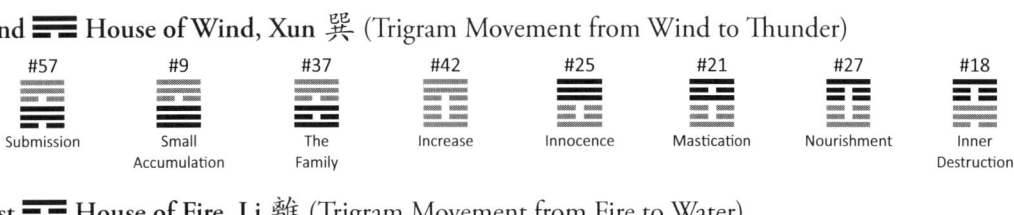

#57	#9	#37	#42	#25	#21	#27	#18
Submission	Small Accumulation	The Family	Increase	Innocence	Mastication	Nourishment	Inner Destruction

1st ☲ House of Fire, Li 離 (Trigram Movement from Fire to Water)

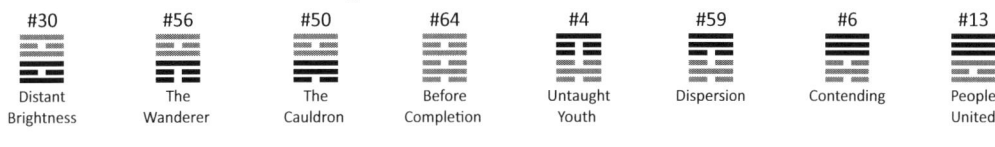

#30	#56	#50	#64	#4	#59	#6	#13
Distant Brightness	The Wanderer	The Cauldron	Before Completion	Untaught Youth	Dispersion	Contending	People United

Book of Sun and Moon

Circular Arrangement of the Eight Gates Eight Houses

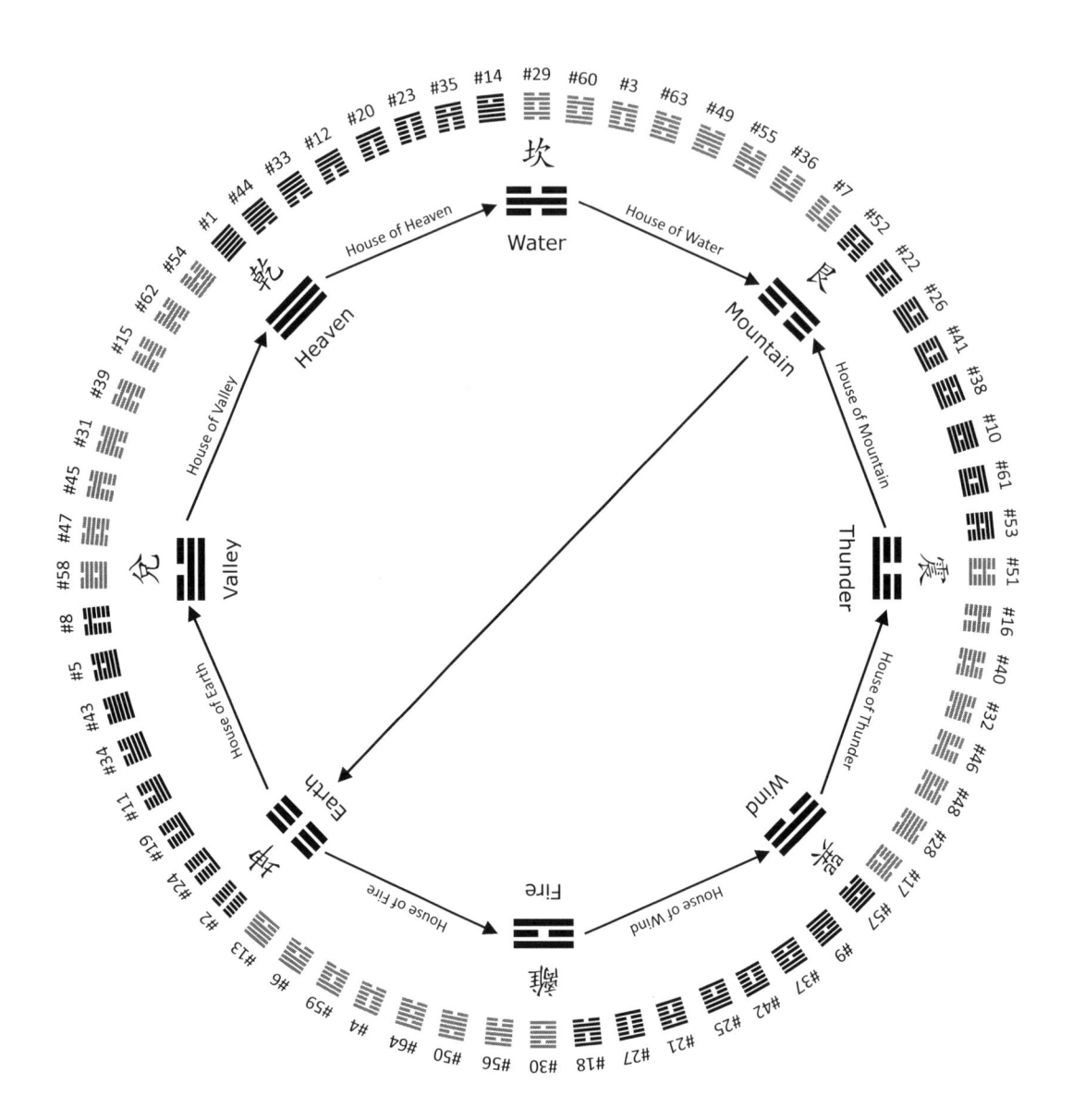

The Eight Houses of the After Heaven Arrangement of Hexagrams

Just as with the houses of the Eight Gates, the After Heaven Eight Houses follow a pattern of changing lines to move through the eight hexagrams of each house.

The *House of Qian,* for example, begins with image #1 *Creativity of Heaven,* which is the image of Heaven ☰ doubled ☰. The other houses start with their respective doubled images as well, with Fire over Fire for the *House of Fire,* Water over Water for the *House of Water,* and so on.

The pattern of changing lines can be seen clearly, for example, by looking at the *House of Qian:*

1st Image	2nd Image	3rd Image	4th Image	5th Image	6th Image	7th Image	8th Image
Heaven Doubled	1st line changed	2nd line changed	3rd line changed	4th line changed	5th line changed	4th line changed	1st–3rd lines changed

Trigram Movement from Heaven to Earth

Note how the upper trigram of Heaven (☰) moves across the top of the hexagrams (as an After Heaven position) until reaching the fourth hexagram/image, where it then changes to its opposite (Earth ☷) in the Before Heaven (lower trigram) position. This Earth trigram then moves across four positions until Heaven (☰) returns as the lower trigram in the eighth hexagram. This identical pattern of trigram movement occurs in all Eight Houses.

Each house also follows the same pattern of changing lines that occurs in the second through seventh images, with the complete change of the lower trigram back to its original starting trigram in the eighth image/position.

Linear-Square Arrangement of the After Heaven Eight Houses

8th ☲ House of Fire, Li 離 (Trigram Movement from Fire to Water)

#30	#56	#50	#64	#4	#59	#6	#13
Distant Brightness	The Wanderer	The Cauldron	Before Completion	Untaught Youth	Dispersion	Contending	People United

7th ☴ House of Wind, Xun 巽 (Trigram Movement from Wind to Thunder)

#57	#9	#37	#42	#25	#21	#27	#18
Submission	Small Accumulation	The Family	Increase	Innocence	Mastication	Nourishment	Inner Destruction

6th ☳ House of Thunder, Zhen 震 (Trigram Movement from Thunder to Wind)

#51	#16	#40	#32	#46	#48	#28	#17
Arousing Movement	Joyful Ease	Liberation	Constancy	Ascending	The Well	Great Passing	Following

5th ☶ House of Mountain, Gen 艮 (Trigram Movement from Mountain to Valley)

#52	#22	#26	#41	#38	#10	#61	#53
Determined Stillness	Adornment	Great Accumulation	Sacrifice	Opposition	Treading	Inner Truth	Gradual Movement

4th ☷ House of Earth, Kun 坤 (Trigram Movement from Earth to Heaven)

#2	#24	#19	#11	#34	#43	#5	#8
Receptivity of Earth	Returning	Approaching	Peacefulness	Great Strength	Decision	Hesitation	Union

3rd ☱ House of Valley, Dui 兌 (Trigram Movement from Valley to Mountain)

#58	#47	#45	#31	#39	#15	#62	#54
Joyousness	Oppression	Collecting	Attraction	Difficult Obstruction	Modesty	Small Passing	Marriageable Maiden

2nd ☰ House of Heaven, Qian 乾 (Trigram Movement from Heaven to Earth)

#1	#44	#33	#12	#20	#23	#35	#14
Creativity of Heaven	Pairing	Retreating	Adversity	Contemplation	Removing	Advancement	Great Possession

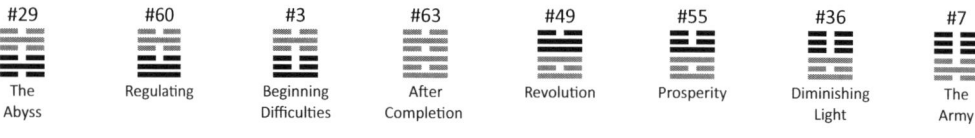

1st ☵ House of Water, Kan 坎 (Trigram Movement from Water to Fire)

#29	#60	#3	#63	#49	#55	#36	#7
The Abyss	Regulating	Beginning Difficulties	After Completion	Revolution	Prosperity	Diminishing Light	The Army

Circular Arrangement of the After Heaven Eight Houses

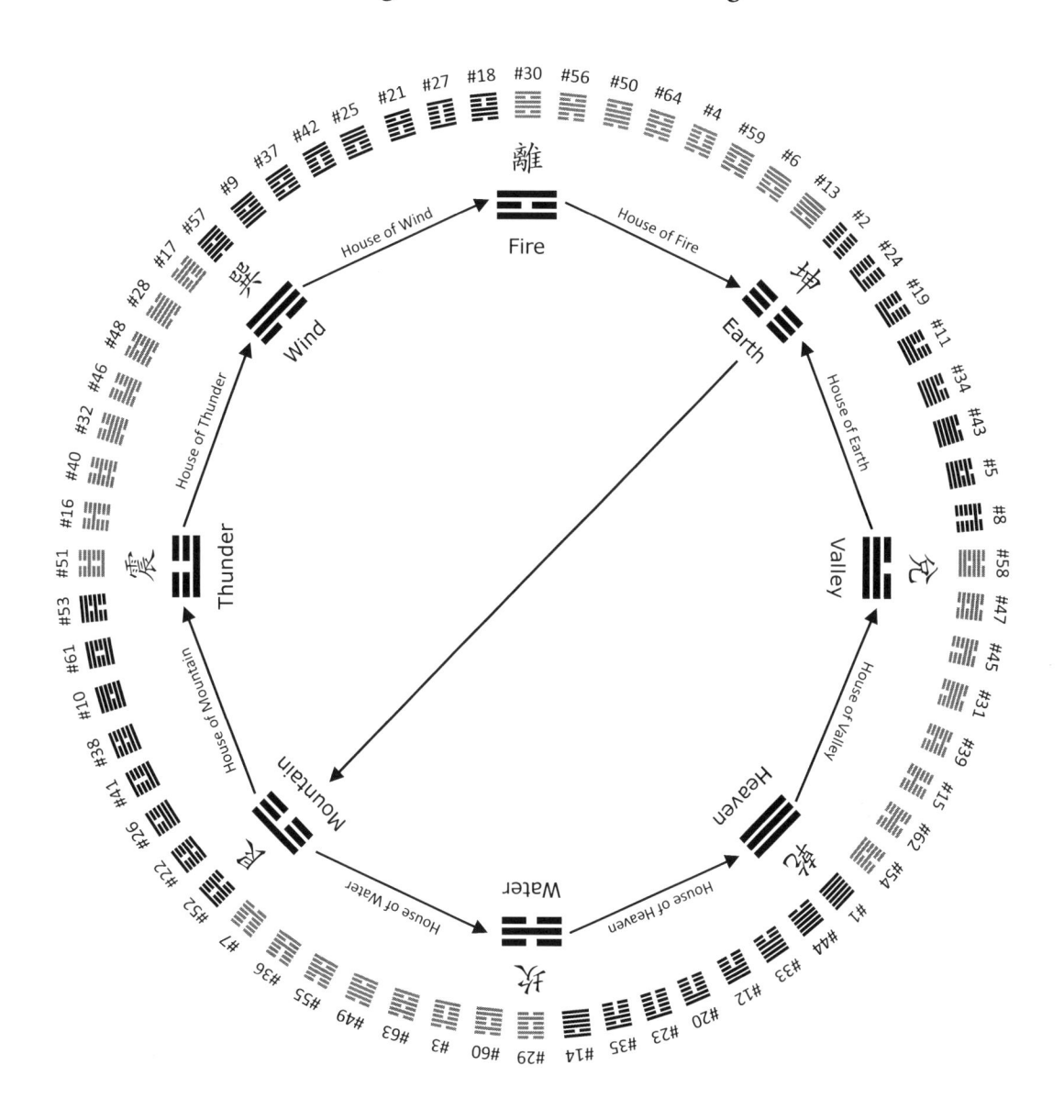

Part Six

Numerological Calculations of the Yi

This section introduces some of the more numerological aspects and correlations of the *Book of Sun and Moon*, including the Ho River Map and Lo River Script, the Nine Palaces, the Sexagenary Cycles (Ten Heavenly Stems and Twelve Earthly Branches), the Twelve Palaces (astrological assignments of the Sixty-Year Hexagram Cycle), Ruling Lines of the hexagrams, the Twelve Sovereign Lunar Hexagrams, and the Eight Positions of the Tai Ji Symbol.

Ho River Map and Lo River Script (河圖洛書, Ho Tu Lo Shu)

These charts in Daoism are usually referred to as the *Remnants of Yu* (禹餘, *Yu Yu*) because Yu the Great's teachings were never fully preserved, and for the most part all that remains of his teachings are contained within these two diagrams. It was Shao Yong who greatly expanded on the ideas of Yu the Great, and King Wen who is said to have used these two diagrams to create the Before Heaven and After Heaven trigram arrangements by transposing the black and white dots into trigrams.

The Lo River Script is a diagram on which the After Heaven Arrangement of the Eight Trigrams are based. The Ho River Map is the diagram showing the production of the Five Elements and their association in creating the Before Heaven Eight Trigrams.[17]

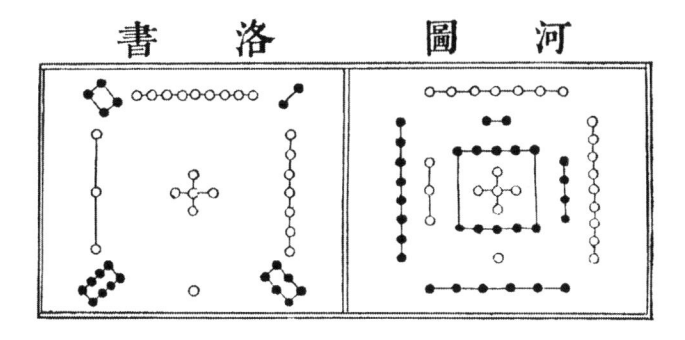

Lo River Script   **Ho River Map**

---

[17] The combined diagram of the Lo River Script and Ho River Map comes from *A Collection on the Essentials of the Rivers He and Luo* (河洛精蘊, *He Luo Jing Yun*).

Lo River Script, Nine Palace Numbers, and After Heaven Trigrams

From the Lo River Script, the Eight Trigrams of the After Heaven Arrangement and Nine Palace numbers were deduced.

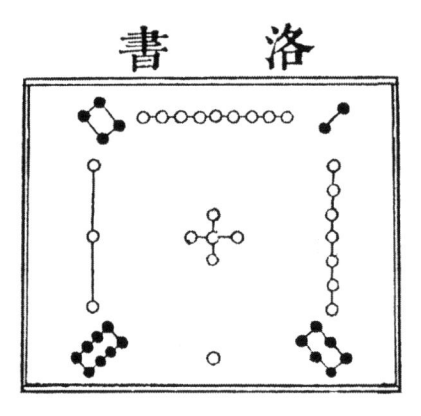

The Nine Palaces Diagram equates to the After Heaven Arrangement of the Eight Trigrams, wherein the numbers in the nine squares match the series of black and white dots that appear in the Lo River Script. The number 4 in the upper left corner of the Nine Palaces Diagram, for example, stands for the square of four black dots that appears in the upper left corner of the Lo River Script. Likewise, in overlapping the After Heaven Trigrams with the Lo River Script, the trigram of Wind appears in the same location. It is the same with the positions of the other series of dots and corresponding trigrams.

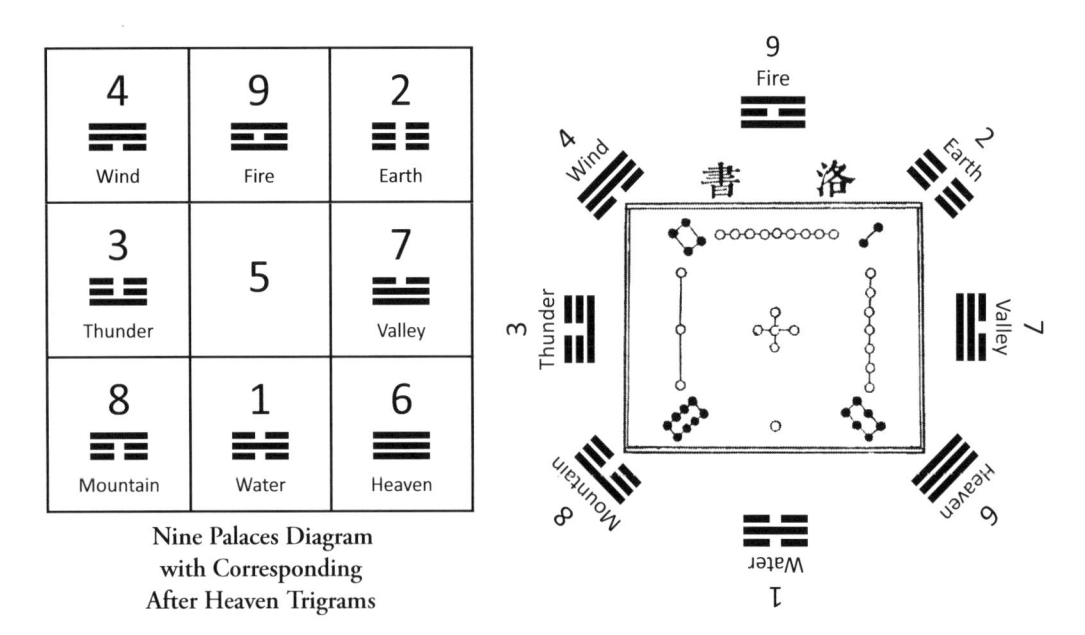

4 Wind	9 Fire	2 Earth
3 Thunder	5	7 Valley
8 Mountain	1 Water	6 Heaven

Nine Palaces Diagram
with Corresponding
After Heaven Trigrams

Ho River Map, Five Elements, Nine Palace Numbers, and Before Heaven Trigrams

From the Ho River Map, the Eight Trigrams of the Before Heaven Arrangement, Five Element production, and Nine Palace numbers were deduced.

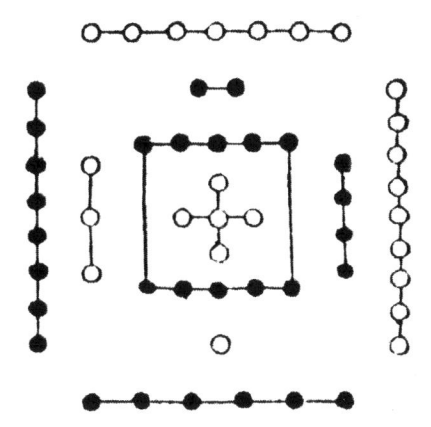

The Ho River Map is somewhat complex and so needs clarification on its meaning and construction. The primary function of the Ho River Map is to show the movements of Production and Completion of the Five Elements. Through this the Nine Palace Numbers are created and the ordering of the Before Heaven Trigrams.

The **8** black dots on the left shows **Thunder** over **Fire**, the **3** white dots. The **8** and **3** represent the **Wood Element** and Eastern direction.

The **6** black dots on the bottom shows **Mountain** over **Earth**, the **1** white dot. The **6** and **1** represent the **Water Element** and the Northern direction.

The **9** white dots on the right side shows **Heaven** over **Valley**, the **4** black dots. The **9** and the **4** represent the **Metal Element** and Western direction.

The **7** white dots on the top shows **Water** over **Wind**, the **2** black dots. The **7** and the **2** represent the **Fire Element** and the Southern direction.

The central **5** white dots and **10** black dots represent the **Earth Element.**

There are **30** black dots and **25** white dots used in the diagram.

> Note: The 30 Completion indications (black dots) when divided by two equals 15, the sum of the Nine Palace Numbers. The 25 Production indications (white dots) when divided by 5 equals 5, the center number of the Nine Palaces Diagram. Also note that the difference between 30 and 25 is 5, which is the difference between the sets of numbers associated with each of the Five Elements.

Number **4** is **Valley**	Number **9** is **Heaven**	Number **2** is **Wind**
Number **3** is **Fire**	Number **5** is **Central**	Number **7** is **Water**
Number **8** is **Thunder**	Number **1** is **Earth**	Number **6** is **Mountain**

Book of Sun and Moon

The center shows 10 black dots and 5 white dots, equaling 15, the sum number of the Nine Palaces.

The white (Production) dots are **Heaven (9), Water (7), Fire (3),** and **Earth (1),** representing the Four Cardinal Directions.

The black (Completion) dots are **Thunder (8), Mountain (6), Valley (4),** and **Wind (2)**, representing the Four Diagonal Directions.

The difference between the Production and Completion numbers is always five (which corresponds with the 5 in the center). So, it can be seen on the bottom of the diagram there is the 1 and 6; on the right side is the 4 and 9; on the top there is the 2 and 7; and on the left side is the 3 and 8. All have a difference of 5.

From this it can be seen that in the Production numbers, the 1 (Earth ☷) produces the 6 (Mountain ☶). The 9 (Heaven ☰) produces the 4 (Valley ☱). The 7 (Water ☵) produces the 2 (Wind ☴). The 3 (Fire ☲) produces the 8 (Thunder ☳).

It can also be viewed in the Completion numbers. The 6 (Mountain ☶) completes the 1 (Earth ☷). The 4 (Valley ☱) completes the 9 (Heaven ☰). The 2 (Wind ☴) completes the 7 (Water ☵). The 8 (Thunder ☳) completes the 3 (Fire ☲).

Also note that in this diagram the 1 white dot is opposite of the 2 black dots, the 3 white dots are opposite of the 4 black ones, the 6 black are opposite of the 7 white, and the 8 black are opposite of the 9 white. The 5 white dots in the center are surrounded by the 10 black dots.

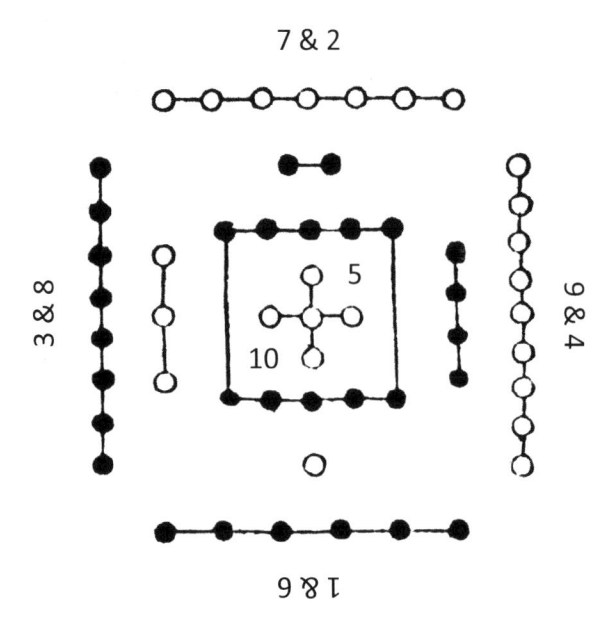

It can also be seen that from the center, the element Earth (the 5 and 10) produces Metal (the 9 and 4). Metal then produces Water (the 1 and 6). Water produces Wood (the 3 and 8). Wood produces Fire (the 7 and 2), and then Fire produces Earth (back to the 5 and 10).

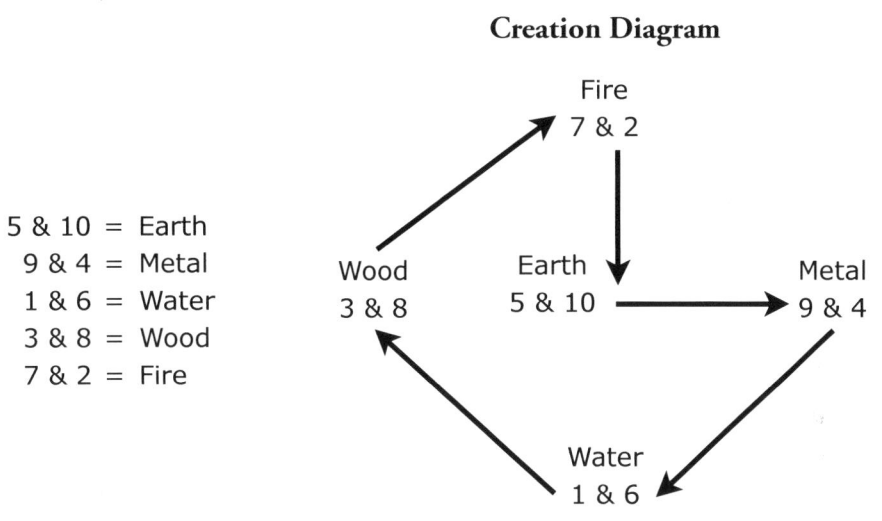

Creation Diagram

5 & 10 = Earth
9 & 4 = Metal
1 & 6 = Water
3 & 8 = Wood
7 & 2 = Fire

Fire
7 & 2

Wood
3 & 8

Earth
5 & 10

Metal
9 & 4

Water
1 & 6

Creating the Before Heaven Trigram Arrangement

Now through the simple placement of the assigned numbers, the Before Heaven trigrams can be positioned. This creation of the Before Heaven Trigram Arrangement is based both upon the number assignments of the Lo River Script and the number assignments of the Ho River Map. Meaning, for example, the number 9 in the Lo River Script assigns Fire to this number, but in the Ho River Map, 9 is assigned to Heaven. So by placing the 9's together there is the placement of Fire (☲) over Heaven (☰), the proper positioning of the trigrams in the Before Heaven and After Heaven arrangements. This pattern and assignment of numbers, then, agrees with all the other numbers and trigrams.

4 ☱ Valley	9 ☲ Heaven	2 ☴ Wind
3 ☳ Fire	5	7 ☵ Water
8 ☶ Thunder	1 ☷ Earth	6 ☶ Mountain

Ho River Map, Diagram of Intercourse of Heaven and Earth

This diagram[18] is another example of the Ho River Map, and is indicating how the Five Elements act as intermediaries between the function and interaction between Heaven and Earth. This diagram, however, explains the Production and Completion numbers through four terms: 1) Ultimate Yin or Yang, 2) Creating Yin or Yang, 3) Completing Yin or Yang, and 4) Old Yin or Yang. Note that in this diagram the center 10 Yin indications (black dots) are placed in a circular manner, which better shows the Yin influence within the diagram.

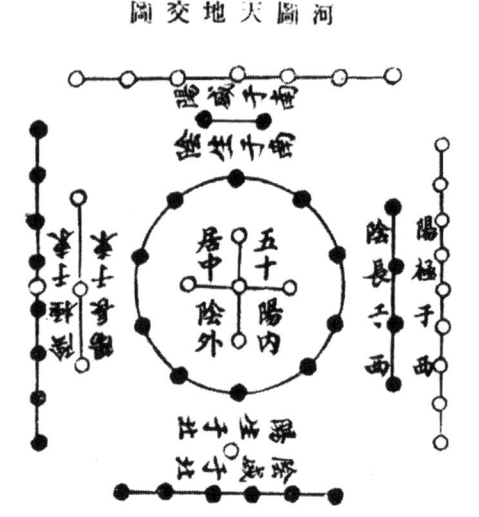

7 White Yang Dots (on top outer)
Completing Yang in the South.

2 Black Yin Dots (on top inner)
Creating Yin in the South.

6 Black Yin Dots (on bottom)
Completing Yin in the North.

1 White Yang Dot (on bottom)
Creating Yang in the North.

9 White Yang Dots (right side)
Ultimate Yang in the West.

4 Black Yin Dots (right side inner)
Old Yin in the West.

8 Black Yin Dots (left side outer)
Ultimate Yin in the East.

3 White Yang Dots (left side inner)
Old Yang in the East.

In the Center:
5 and **10** (五十) are in the Central Position (居中)
  Yang is internal (陽內)
    [5 White Yin Dots]
  Yin is external (陰外)
    [10 Black Yin Dots]

---

[18] From *Tai Ji Quan Illustrated and Explained* (太極拳圖說, *Tai Ji Quan Tu Shuo*) by Chen Pinsan, edited by Chen Panling.

Meaning of the Eight Terms:

- ☰ 9 (Heaven) is called **Ultimate Yang** (太陽, Tai Yang) because all three lines are Yang.
- ☱ 4 (Valley) is called **Old Yin** (老陰, Lao Yin) because of the top Yin line.
- ☲ 3 (Fire) is called **Old Yang** (老陽, Lao Yang) because of the Yin line between the two Yang lines.
- ☳ 8 (Thunder) is called **Ultimate Yin** (太陰, Tai Yin) because of the two Yin lines atop a Yang line.
- ☴ 2 (Wind) is called **Creating Yin** (少陰, Shao Yin, Young Yin) because of the one Yin line on the bottom.
- ☵ 7 (Water) is called **Completing Yang** (中陽, Zhong Yang, Central Yang) because of the Yang line in the center of the trigram.
- ☶ 6 (Mountain) is called **Completing Yin** (中陰, Zhong Yin, Central Yin) because of the two bottom Yin lines.
- ☷ 1 (Earth) is called **Creating Yang** (少陽, Shao Yang, Young Yang) because the three Yin lines will change to Yang, reverting to Heaven. (Yin at its extreme reverts to Yang.)

The Eight Terms in the Before and After Heaven Trigram Arrangements

When viewed in the Before and After Heaven configurations, the Eight Terms reveal a variety of relationships between the BH and AH trigrams.

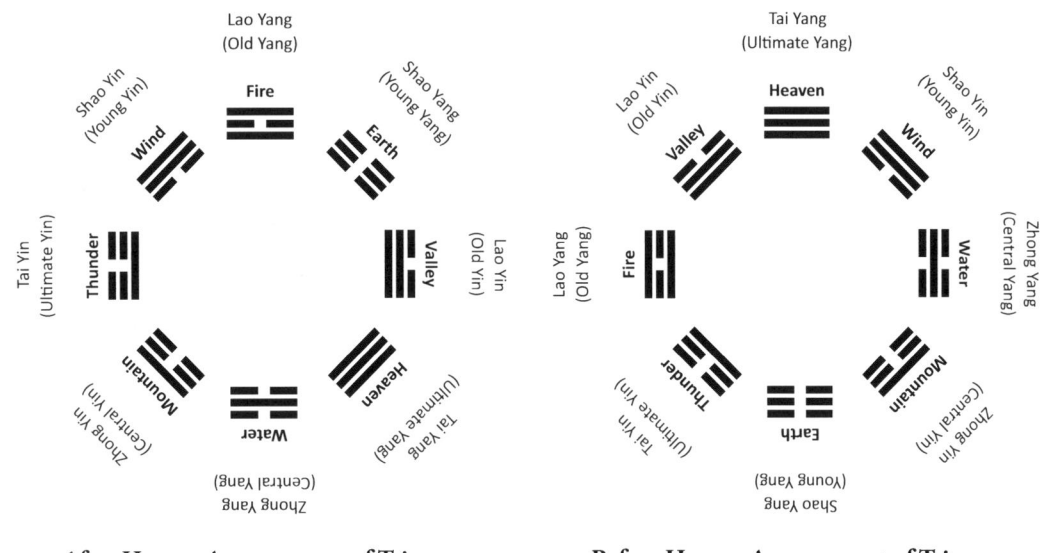

After Heaven Arrangement of Trigrams with Corresponding Eight Terms

Before Heaven Arrangement of Trigrams with Corresponding Eight Terms

Ho River Map and Tai Ji Diagram

This illustration shows the circular movement of the series of dots from the Ho River Map through the Tai Ji Symbol.[19] The white spaces are Yang and contain the white dots of 9, 7, 3, and 1 that wind around into the center of the 5 white Yang circles. In the black spaces are the Yin circles of 8, 6, 4, and 2, which wind around into the center of the two sets of 5 black dots. The center area shows 15 dots—10 Yin and 5 Yang. There are 25 Yang white dots, and 30 Yin black dots (counting the dots in the black areas).

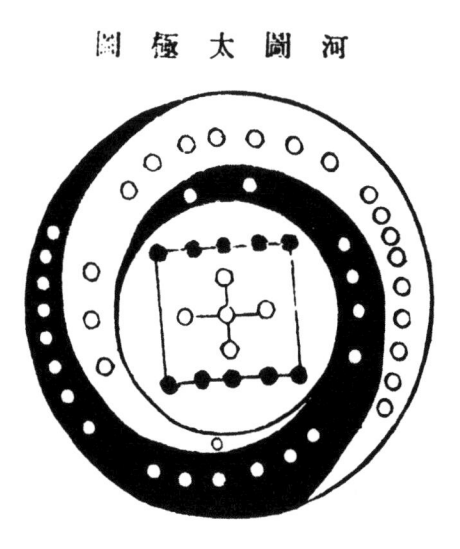

The Nine Palaces (九宮, Jiu Gong)

The origin of the Nine Palaces numerology appears to have begun when Yu the Great had divided his kingdom in China (the North, East, and Central areas of China) into nine separate provinces, which then led to dividing properties and lands into nine sections. He also had nine cauldrons made from the best metals from each province. These nine cauldrons were later used symbolically in Daoism as the Nine Stages of Cultivation. From this method of dividing provinces and properties into nine sections the entire system of Feng Shui (風水, Wind and Water) began to develop—everything from designing interiors of a home to physiognomy. From Yu the Great's creation of the Ho River Map and Lo River Script, the neo-Confucian Shao Yong created the method of

---

19 From *Tai Ji Quan Illustrated and Explained* (太極拳圖說, *Tai Ji Quan Tu Shuo*) by Chen Pinsan, edited by Chen Panling.

Plum Blossom Numerology of the *Book of Changes*,[20] and this then became one of the original writings on the art of Feng Shui.

The Magic Square (not a Chinese term) is properly called the Nine Palaces Diagram (九宮圖, Jiu Gong Tu). The original Ho River Map used the number six as the central number, and all other numbers add up to eighteen. This may have been an equation wherein the six represents the number of lines in a hexagram, and the eighteen shows the number of changes needed in sorting the stalks to create a hexagram. Only three numbers can be used to arrive at eighteen, which may be another representation of the three sortings to arrive at one line in a casting (see Part Eight, p. 123).

There are two manners of calculating the Nine Palaces. One comes from the original (Fu Xi) arrangement of the Eight Trigrams and the other from the newer (King Wen) versions, which rely heavily on the After Heaven Arrangement of the Eight Trigrams.

Both Nine Palaces Diagrams contain eight possible variants of three numbers (in columns, rows, and diagonal directions) that add up to either eighteen in the original diagram or that add up to fifteen in the later version. The older version of the Nine Palaces Diagram relates to the significance of the number three (in the three sortings of the stalks in casting one line of an image) and six (representing the six lines of a hexagram).

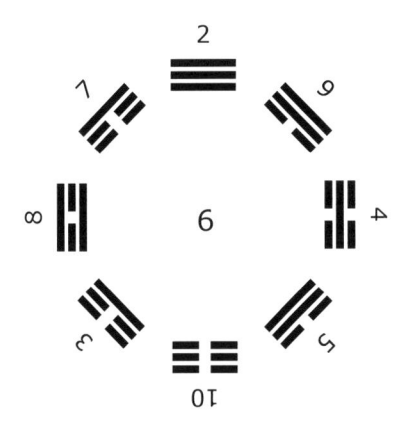

Nine Palaces Diagram Corresponding with the Original Arrangement of Eight Trigrams

7	2	9
8	6	4
3	10	5

Each column, row, and diagonal direction adds up to eighteen.

Original Arrangement of Trigrams with Nine Palace Numbers

---

20 See *I Ching Numerology: Based on Shao Yung's Classic Plum Blossom Numerology* by Da Liu (HarperCollins, 1979). This book is still the most authoritative work on this subject in English.

Book of Sun and Moon

**After Heaven Trigram Arrangement
with Nine Palace Numbers**

**Before Heaven Trigram Arrangement
with Nine Palace Numbers**

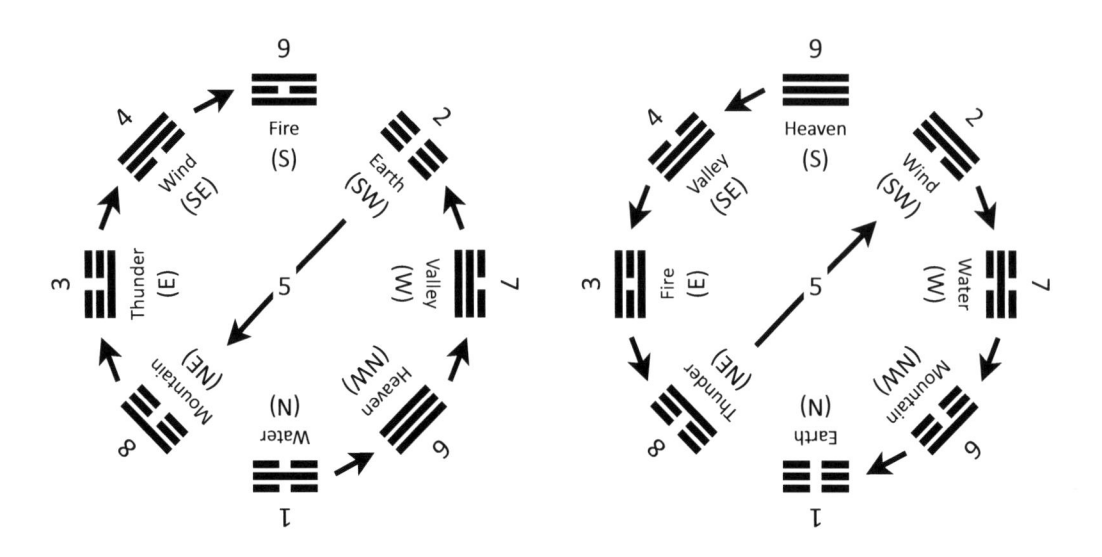

**Nine Palaces Diagram Corresponding
with the Before and After Heaven Trigrams**

4	9	2
3	5	7
8	1	6

Each column, row, and diagonal direction
adds up to fifteen.

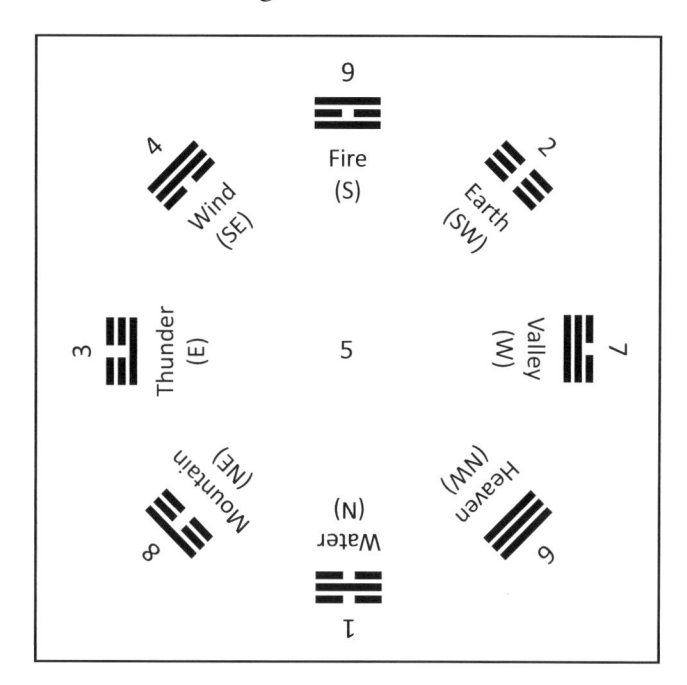

After Heaven Arrangement and Nine Palace Numbers

Correlations of the After Heaven Trigrams and Nine Palace Numerology

1 (Kan, Water ☵) is associated with a person's livelihood and career.
   Supported by Before Heaven image of Kun (☷ Earth) in the North.

6 (Qian, Heaven ☰) is associated with friends and travel.
   Supported by Before Heaven image of Gen (☶ Mountain) in the Northwest.

7 (Dui, Valley ☱) is associated with children and creativity.
   Supported by Before Heaven image of Kan (☵ Water) in the West.

2 (Kun, Earth ☷) is associated with relationships and love.
   Supported by Before Heaven image of Xun (☴ Wind) in the Southwest.

8 (Gen, Mountain ☶) is associated with skills and knowledge.
   Supported by Before Heaven image of Zhen (☳ Thunder) in the Northeast.

3 (Zhen, Thunder ☳) is associated with family and business.
   Supported by Before Heaven image of Li (☲ Fire) in the East.

4 (Xun, Wind ☴) is associated with wealth and prosperity.
   Supported by Before Heaven image of Dui (☱ Valley) in the Southeast.

9 (Li, Fire ☲) is associated with fame and reputation.
   Supported by Before Heaven image of Qian (☰ Heaven) in the South.

Lo River Script, the Diagram of Intercourse Between Sun and Moon[21]

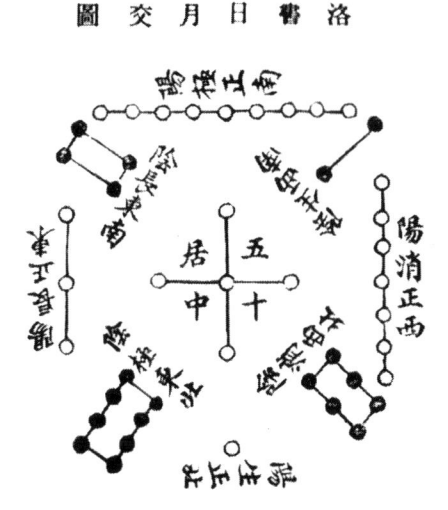

洛書日月交圖

9 White Yang [Sun] Circles: Ultimate Yang of the Cardinal South
> [The father acquires the 9 in Qian of Heaven and Sky]

4 Black Yin [Moon] Circles: Old Yin of the Southeast
> [The youngest female acquires the 4 in Dui of Valley and Lake]

3 White Yang [Sun] Circles: Old Yang of the Cardinal East
> [The middle female acquires the 3 in Li of Brightness and Fire]

8 Black Yin [Moon] Circles: Ultimate Yin of the Northeast
> [The eldest male acquires the 8 in Zhen of Lightning and Thunder]

1 White Yang [Sun] Circle: Yang is born in the Cardinal North
> [The mother acquires the 1 in Kun of Receptiveness and Earth]

6 Black Yin [Moon] Circles: Pure Yin of the Northwest
> [The youngest male acquires the 6 in Gen of Stillness and Mountain]

7 White Yang [Sun] Circles: Pure Yang of the Cardinal West
> [The middle female acquires the 7 in Kan of the Abyss and Water]

2 Black Yin [Moon] Circles: Yin is born in the Southwest
> [The eldest female acquires the 2 in Xun of Gentleness and Wind]

In the center of the diagram it reads, "The 5 and 10 Central Positions." The five white dots represent the Yang aspects of the Five Elements. The 10 refers to ten Yin blacks dots normally placed in these diagrams (as in the Ho River Map), but were left out here.

---

21 From *Tai Ji Quan Illustrated and Explained* (太極拳圖說, *Tai Ji Quan Tu Shuo*) by Chen Pinsan, edited by Chen Panling.

The Sexagenary Cycles (六十花甲, Liu Shi Hua Jia)

Literally translating as "The Sixty Stems and Blossoms," the Sexagenary Cycles are based on the calculations of the Ten Heavenly Stems and Twelve Earthly Branches. The Ten Heavenly Stems were formed on the Yin and Yang aspects of the Five Elements (五行, Wu Xing), equaling ten divisions, and the Twelve Earthly Branches on the Twelve Moons of the year and the Twelve Astrological Animal Signs. The joining of these two systems are what comprise the Chinese calendar.

The Ten Heavenly Stems (十天干, Shi Tian Gan)

The Ten Heavenly, or Celestial, Stems first appeared in the Shang dynasty (1766–1154 BCE) as ordinal numbers for the ten days of the week (as they were counted then) and to determine specific days for making offerings and sacrifices to the dead. Over time, the ten symbols were combined with the Twelve Earthly Branches to calculate a sixty-year cyclical calendar that is still in use today.

The Ten Heavenly Stems are the Yin and Yang components of the Five Elements of Earth (土, Tu), Metal (金, Jin), Water (水, Shui), Wood (木, Mu), and Fire (火, Huo). Each element, then, can be either Yin or Yang, and this is what makes ten separate classifications or Stems. Those who practice Feng Shui or Chinese Astrology must be well versed in their knowledge of the Ten Heavenly Stems. Each Stem is not only showing a characteristic of the Five Elements and Five Planets, but likewise goes into descriptions of personality traits for those born under a particular Stem. Just as the animal signs (Twelve Earthly Branches) can describe a person's characteristics, the Ten Heavenly Stems provide an ever deeper description, and this is why they became such an important part of Chinese astrology.

Here is a brief summary of the Stems and their meanings on nature:

First Stem: **Yang Wood** (甲, Jia) is likened to the forests and trees in nature.
Second Stem: **Yin Wood** (乙, Yi) is likened to plants and flowers.
Third Stem: **Yang Fire** (丙, Bing) is likened to the Sun.
Fourth Stem: **Yin Fire** (丁, Ding) is likened to fires and flames.
Fifth Stem: **Yang Earth** (戊, Wu) is likened to the boulders and rocks.
Sixth Stem: **Yin Earth** (己, Ji) is likened to soil and farmed fields.
Seventh Stem: **Yang Metal** (庚, Geng) is likened to steel and swords.
Eighth Stem: **Yin Metal** (辛, Xin) is likened to gold and silver.
Ninth Stem: **Yang Water** (壬, Ren) is likened to rivers and oceans.
Tenth Stem: **Yin Water** (癸, Gui) is likened to rain and dew.

The Twelve Earthly Branches (十二地支, Shi Er Di Zhi)

The Twelve Earthly Branches[22] are correlations to the months of a year and to the twelve two-hour periods of the day. These twelve divisions were originally calculated by Chinese astrologers observing the orbit of Jupiter (歲星, Sui Xing), which took twelve years to completely orbit the Earth. Thus, they were able to identify twelve months, twelve double-hours of the day, and even the 120 minutes within the double hour. The Earthly Branches also date back to the Shang dynasty, but originally they were not part of calendar calculation. This was solely done through the Ten Heavenly Stems, as it was the ritual calendar for the imperials of those times. When the astrological correlations began to gain popularity, however, the two systems came together to calculate the sixty-year cycles of time, a simple formula of 5 (Five Elements) x 12 (Earthly Branches).

Twelve Earthly Branches	Twelve Hours	Twelve Astrological Animals	Twelve Months
子, Zi	11:00 p.m. to 1:00 a.m.	Rat (鼠, Shu)	11
丑, Chou	1:00 a.m. to 3:00 a.m.	Ox (牛, Niu)	12
寅, Yin	3:00 a.m. to 5:00 a.m.	Tiger (虎, Hu)	1
卯, Mao	5:00 a.m. to 7:00 a.m.	Rabbit (兔, Tu)	2
辰, Chen	7:00 a.m. to 9:00 a.m.	Dragon (龍, Long)	3
巳, Si	9:00 a.m. to 11:00 a.m.	Snake (蛇, She)	4
午, Wu	11:00 a.m. to 1:00 p.m.	Horse (馬, Ma)	5
未, Wei	1:00 p.m. to 3:00 p.m.	Goat (羊, Yang)	6
申, Shen	3:00 p.m. to 5:00 p.m.	Monkey (猴, Hou)	7
酉, You	5:00 p.m. to 7:00 p.m.	Rooster (雞, Ji)	8
戌, Xu	7:00 p.m. to 9:00 p.m.	Dog (狗, Gou)	9
亥, Hai	9:00 p.m. to 11:00 p.m.	Pig (猪, Zhu)	10

---

22   Like the term *Stem*, "Branch" likewise relates to the branches of a plant or tree. Using these terms may seem confusing, but the idea is clearer if Stems are thought of as Celestial Stems, which connect to Heaven. Branches are termed Earthly Branches to imply the connection to Earth. Thus the two systems of calculation have to do with a human being's connection to Heaven and Earth, as shown with the Three Powers of Heaven, Humanity, and Earth.

The Twelve Palaces (十二宮, Shi Er Gong)

The Twelve Palaces is a term used to describe the Twelve Equatorial Constellations of the Zodiac and is correlated with the Twelve Astrological Animal Signs[23] and the Twelve Earthly Branches. Astrology in China definitely incorporated the images of the *Book of Sun and Moon* to further its depth and meaning, and from this astrology all calculations of the Ten Heavenly Stems and Twelve Earthly Branches can be interpreted and correlated into a hexagram.

For example,

> Every Sixty-Year Cycle begins in a **Wood Rat Year**
> (or the **Jia Zi** Year), which is image #47 *Oppression* (困, Kun).
> > **Jia** 甲 is the first of the **Ten Heavenly Stems** and is correlated with the element of **Wood** (木, Mu).
> > **Zi** 子 is the first of the **Twelve Earthly Branches** and is correlated with the animal sign of **Rat** (鼠, Shu).

> All Sixty-Year Cycles end in a **Water Pig Year**
> (or the **Gui Hai** Year), which is image #32 *Constancy* (恒, Heng).
> > **Gui** 癸 is the last of the **Ten Heavenly Stems** and is correlated with the element of **Water** (水, Shui).
> > **Hai** 亥 is the last of the **Twelve Earthly Branches** and is correlated with the animal sign of the **Pig** (猪, Zhu).

---

23   Illustration from *I Ching: Taoist Book of Days 1981* by Khigh Alx Dhiegh (Ballantine, 1980).

The Sixty-Year Cycle of Hexagrams

As can be seen in the chart on the following page, this arrangement of hexagrams can be read in a number of ways. Each row, for example, represents one of the Five Elements, and two Heavenly Stems. Each column equates to an Earthly Branch and corresponding astrological animal sign. The years in the cycle follow a diagonal pattern of moving through the arrangement. Reading from right to left in pairs, each set advances throughout the arrangement by descending through the rows in a diagonal, or spiraling, fashion (see the "Years in Cycle" rows in the chart on the following page).

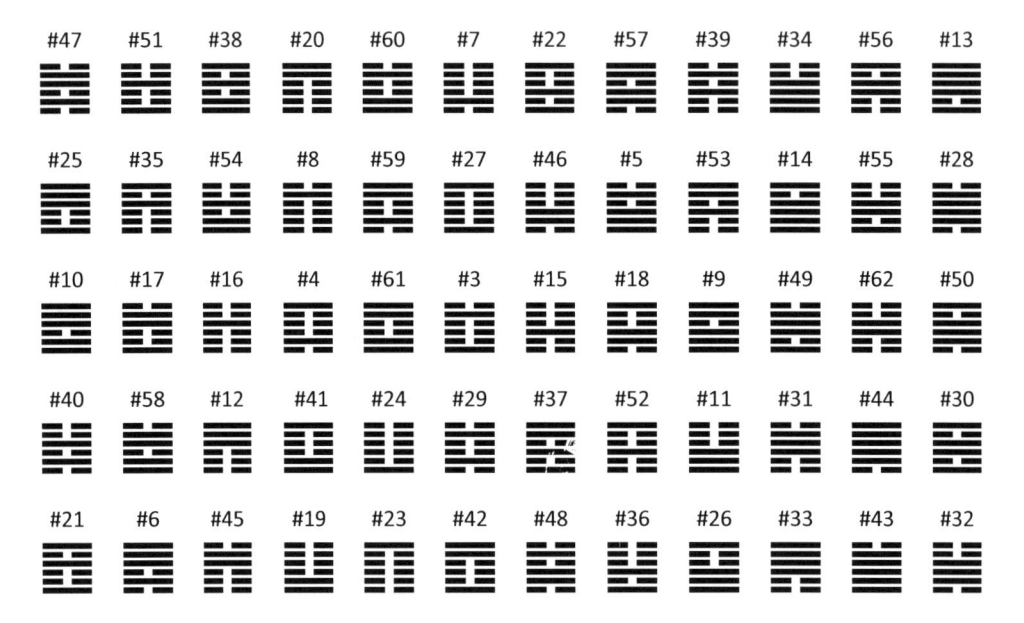

#47	#51	#38	#20	#60	#7	#22	#57	#39	#34	#56	#13
#25	#35	#54	#8	#59	#27	#46	#5	#53	#14	#55	#28
#10	#17	#16	#4	#61	#3	#15	#18	#9	#49	#62	#50
#40	#58	#12	#41	#24	#29	#37	#52	#11	#31	#44	#30
#21	#6	#45	#19	#23	#42	#48	#36	#26	#33	#43	#32

Determining the Four Pillars and Life Path Hexagrams

The term "Four Pillars" (四柱, Si Zhu) comes from the Studies of the Four Pillars of Destiny Principles (四柱命理學, Si Zhu Ming Li Yue). It is also connected to the Chinese phrase *The Eight Characters of Birth Time* (生辰八字, Sheng Chen Ba Zi), more commonly just called the *Eight Characters* (八字, Ba Zi). This term "Eight Characters" is used because in the process of determining the Four Pillar Birth Hexagrams, eight characters (four Heavenly Stems and four Earthly Branches) are produced. This process is all based on a person's year, month, day, and hour of birth, wherein each period is represented by a hexagram (or Pillar).

From the charts of the Ten Heavenly Stems and Twelve Earthly Branches, along with the correlation of the Twelve Astrological Animal Signs and corresponding Sixty-Year-Cycle Hexagram, the Eight Characters (Heavenly Stems and Earthly Branches) and Four Destiny Symbols (corresponding Pillar Hexagrams) for any date can be determined.

Combined Chart of the Ten Heavenly Stems, Twelve Earthly Branches, Twelve Animals, Five Elements, and the Sixty-Year Cycle of Hexagrams[24]

Earthly Branches	1 Zi 子	2 Chou 丑	3 Yin 寅	4 Mao 卯	5 Chen 辰	6 Si 巳	7 Wu 午	8 Wei 未	9 Shen 申	10 You 酉	11 Xu 戌	12 Hai 亥
Twelve Animals	Rat 鼠 Shu	Ox 牛 Niu	Tiger 虎 Hu	Rabbit 兔 Tu	Dragon 龍 Long	Snake 蛇 She	Horse 馬 Ma	Goat 羊 Yang	Monkey 猴 Hou	Rooster 雞 Ji	Dog 狗 Gou	Pig 猪 Zhu
Heavenly Stems												
Wood (木, Mu) 1) Jia (甲) 2) Yi (乙)	#47	#51	#38	#20	#60	#7	#22	#57	#39	#34	#56	#13
Years in Cycle	(1st)	(2nd)	(51st)	(52nd)	(41st)	(42nd)	(31st)	(32nd)	(21st)	(22nd)	(11th)	(12th)
Present Era	1984	1985	2034	2035	2024	2025	2014	2015	2004	2005	1994	1995
Fire (火, Huo) 3) Bing (丙) 4) Ding (丁)	#25	#35	#54	#8	#59	#27	#46	#5	#53	#14	#55	#28
Years in Cycle	(13th)	(14th)	(3rd)	(4th)	(53rd)	(54th)	(43rd)	(44th)	(33rd)	(34th)	(23rd)	(24th)
Present Era	1996	1997	1986	1987	2036	2037	2026	2027	2016	2017	2006	2007
Earth (土, Tu) 5) Wu (戊) 6) Ji (己)	#10	#17	#16	#4	#61	#3	#15	#18	#9	#49	#62	#50
Years in Cycle	(25th)	(26th)	(15th)	(16th)	(5th)	(6th)	(55th)	(56th)	(45th)	(46th)	(35th)	(36th)
Present Era	2008	2009	1998	1999	1988	1989	2038	2039	2028	2029	2018	2019
Metal (金, Jin) 7) Geng (庚) 8) Xin (辛)	#40	#58	#12	#41	#24	#29	#37	#52	#11	#31	#44	#30
Years in Cycle	(37th)	(38th)	(27th)	(28th)	(17th)	(18th)	(7th)	(8th)	(57th)	(58th)	(47th)	(48th)
Present Era	2020	2021	2010	2011	2000	2001	1990	1991	2040	2041	2030	2031
Water (水, Shui) 9) Ren (壬) 10) Gui (癸)	#21	#6	#45	#19	#23	#42	#48	#36	#26	#33	#43	#32
Years in Cycle	(49th)	(50th)	(39th)	(40th)	(29th)	(30th)	(19th)	(20th)	(9th)	(10th)	(59th)	(60th)
Present Era	2032	2033	2022	2023	2012	2013	2002	2003	1992	1993	2042	2043

[24] Hexagrams associated with Yang years (the odd-numbered columns of Earthly Branches) appear in the lighter color. Yin years appear in black (the even-numbered columns of Earthly Branches). Note that these color associations are not related to the hexagrams' Sun or Moon designations, which may be in either color. The years running from 1984 to 2043 represent the present-era Sixty-Year Cycle. The "Years in Cycle" numbers indicate the year position of each hexagram within the Sixty-Year Cycle (Hexagram #54, for example, is always the third year of the Sixty-Year Cycle). This is the same with the other hexagrams being the same year in every cycle. The Heavenly Stems are grouped by their elements, with the odd-numbered stems being Yang, and the even-numbered stems being Yin.

If, for example, a person was born on April 5, 1962, at 10:00 a.m., his or her *Ba Zi* would be calculated as follows:[25]

Year
The year 1962 is **Ren Yin** (壬寅), the Stem and Branch signs of a **Yang Water Tiger,** symbolized by **#45** *Collecting* (Valley over Earth)

Moon
April of that year is **Jia Chen** (甲辰), Stem and Branch signs of a **Yang Wood Dragon,** symbolized by **#60** *Regulating* (Water over Valley)

Day
April 5th is **Gui You** (癸酉), Stem and Branch of a **Yin Water Rooster,** symbolized by **#33** *Retreating* (Heaven over Mountain)

Hour
Time of birth is 10:00 a.m., which falls into the hour of **Ding Si** (丁巳), Stem and Branch of a **Yin Fire Snake,** symbolized by image **#27** *Nourishment* (Mountain over Thunder)

From these Four Pillar hexagrams a person's Life Path[26] or Destiny Hexagram can then be calculated. A Life Path Hexagram shows the path a person should follow to fulfill his or her destiny in the best way possible. The next step, then, is to first calculate the Before Heaven and After Heaven Destiny hexagrams. This is done by taking the top (Yang, or Sun) trigrams from the Year and Day to determine the Before Heaven Destiny Hexagram, which, in this case, would be Valley over Heaven, **#43** *Decision:*

Before Heaven Destiny Hexagram

---

[25] To find the Eight Characters for any date, please visit the Sanctuary of Dao's website (see its Calendar page) to use an online *Four Pillar Solar Calendar Converter.* Since this app uses the Solar Calendar, however, check the Lunar Chart PDFs for any potential difference in the Heavenly Stem and Earthly Branch characters associated with the given year and month, as these can differ between Solar and Lunar calendars. Characters for the day and hour, however, will be the same.

[26] See the forthcoming book *Chinese Astrology* by Stuart Alve Olson and Amy Searcy for a fuller description of this process.

Then determine the After Heaven Destiny Hexagram by taking the top two trigrams from the Moon (month) and Hour hexagrams. This then shows Water over Mountain, *#39 Difficult Obstruction:*

After Heaven Destiny Hexagram

Lastly, to determine the Life Path Hexagram, take the upper inner trigram from the BH Destiny Hexagram, which is Heaven, and the lower inner trigram from the AH Destiny Hexagram, which is Water. Placing the Sun (upper) trigram of Heaven over the Moon (lower) trigram of Water then creates hexagram *#6 Contending*, the person's Life Path Hexagram.

Life Path Hexagram

Once a Life Path Hexagram is calculated, the image's Associated Developed Hexagrams can be examined to discover further meanings and correlations of that image. (See *Book of Sun and Moon*, volume II, for information on each individual hexagram.)

Note that in the above determinations of the Before Heaven and After Heaven Destiny hexagrams the upper trigram is always used, not the lower trigram. In the calculation of the Four Pillars, the hexagrams are determined first by the lower trigram and then the upper trigram, a Before Heaven configuration (based on Shao Yong's teachings), or, in another view, an ascending development of the trigrams.

In configuring the Life Path Hexagram, however, the upper trigrams are used, an After Heaven configuration, or descending development of the trigrams. It can also be said that the Four Birth Hexagrams are determined on their Before Heaven (primordial) conditions, and Life Path Hexagrams are determined on After Heaven (temporal) conditions.

Ruling Lines (君爻, Jun Yao)

Wang Bi or Shao Yong assigned Ruling Lines to each of the Sixty-Four Hexagrams, which indicate where the power and influence of a hexagram resides. Ruling Lines are also arranged in correlation with the After Heaven trigrams. In hexagram #1 ䷀, for example, the Ruling Line is the fifth Yang line, and in hexagram #2 ䷁, the Ruling Line is the second Yin line.

In image #1, if the Yang Ruling Line is changed to Yin, the image changes to Fire over Heaven ䷍ (#14 *Great Possession*), which happens to be exactly the hexagram revealed at the top of the Before and After Heaven Trigram arrangements in their starting configurations (see highlighted trigrams in the circular graphic below). In image #2, if the Ruling Line, second Yin line, is changed to Yang, this then creates the image of Earth over Water ䷆ (#7 *The Army*), which can also be seen at the bottom of the graphic.

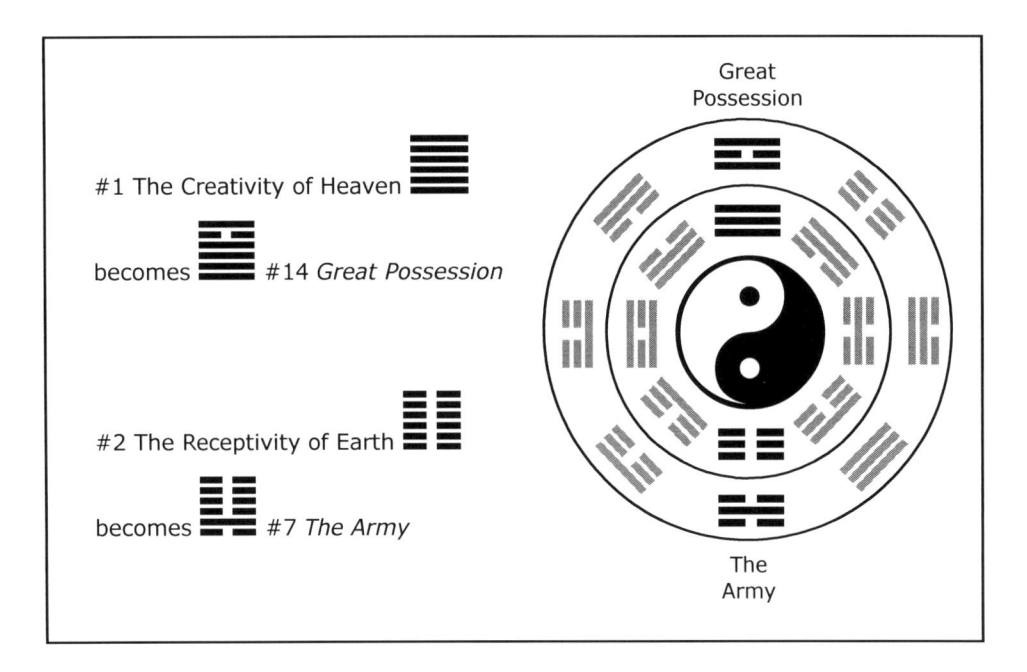

Sovereign Hexagrams of the Calendar

In the *Zhou Yi Cantong Qi* by Wei Boyang appears the construct and explanation of what is called the "Twelve Sovereign Images" (辟卦, Bi Gua). These images, as Wei Boyang relates, are the movements of the Sun and Moon throughout the year, and he likewise states that there are six trigrams relating to the days within a month showing the ascent and descent of the Sun and Moon.

The Twelve Lunar Sovereign Hexagrams

	#24	#19	#11	#34	#43	#1	#44	#33	#12	#20	#23	#2
	Fu	Lin	Tai	Da Zhuang	Guai	Qian	Gou	Dun	Pi	Guan	Bo	Kun
Earthly Branch	子 Zi	丑 Chou	寅 Yin	卯 Mao	辰 Chen	巳 Si	午 Wu	未 Wei	申 Shen	酉 You	戌 Xu	亥 Hai
Twelve Animals	Rat	Ox	Tiger	Rabbit	Dragon	Snake	Horse	Goat	Monkey	Rooster	Dog	Pig
Month	11	12	1	2	3	4	5	6	7	8	9	10
Hour	23-1	1-3	3-5	5-7	7-9	9-11	11-13	13-15	15-17	17-19	19-21	21-23

After Heaven Arrangement of the Sixty-Four Hexagrams

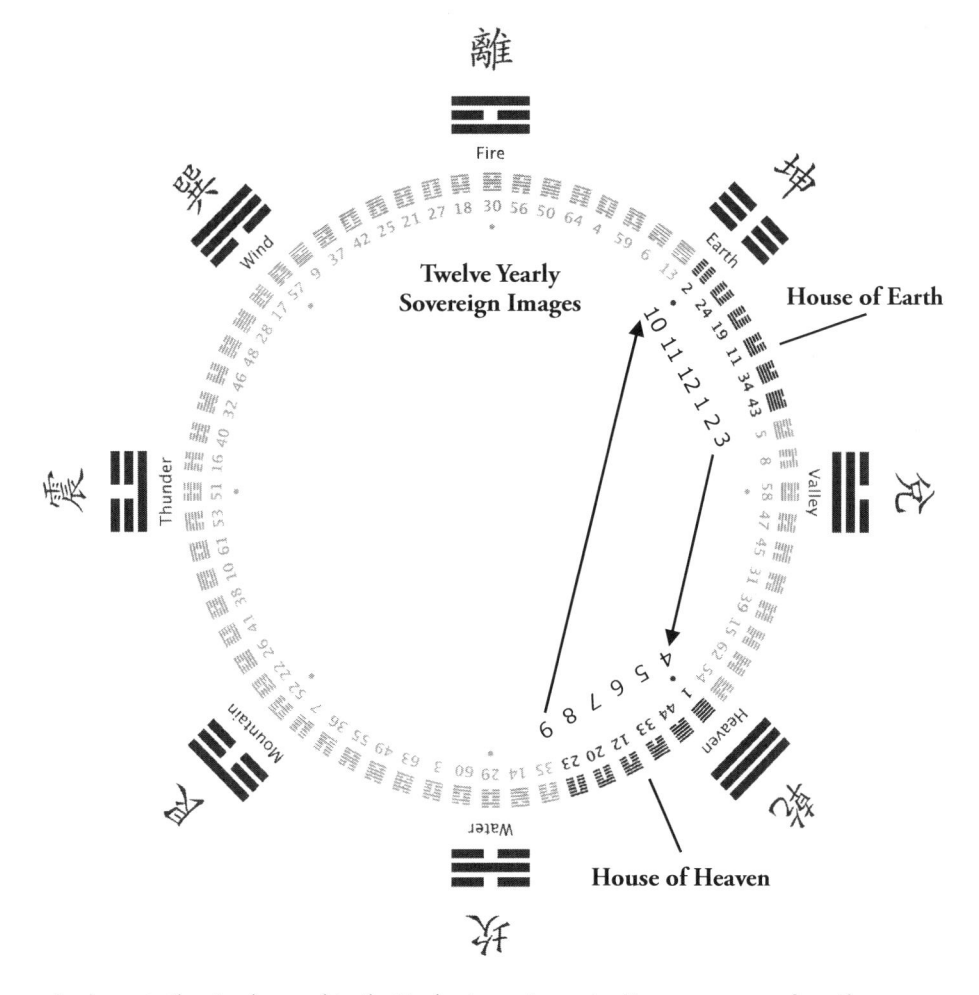

As shown in the circular graphic, the Twelve Lunar Sovereign Hexagrams come from the houses of Heaven and Earth in the After Heaven Arrangement of the Sixty-Four Hexagrams.

```
                          The Six Lunar Images

        ☳          ☱          ☰          ☴          ☶          ☷
       Zhen        Dui        Qian        Xun        Gen        Kun
        震          兌          乾          巽          艮          坤

                    ☲                                  ☵
                    Li                                 Kan
                    離                                  坎

            Sun Images                            Moon Images
```

In the Six Lunar Images, this particular sequence of trigrams illustrates the ascent of Yang (or Sun) lines and the descent of Yin (or Moon) lines throughout the thirty days of a lunar month. Note that the images of Li (Fire ☲) and Kan (Water ☵) are not included. Fire represents the Sun, and Water represents the Moon, and these are the images ascending (Fire, Yang) and descending (Water, Yin) through the other six images.

The Eight Positions of the Before Heaven and After Heaven Arrangements in Correlation with the Supreme Ultimate Symbol

When the Tai Ji (Supreme Ultimate) Symbol is rotated through the eight positions of the Before Heaven Arrangement, it carries the BH trigrams with it. However, when the Tai Ji Symbol and the BH trigrams are moved to a new position, the After Heaven trigrams remain in their fixed position on the outside circle. This particular function is quite involved and not necessary for the intent of this work. Suffice to say that the various configurations factor into the ordering of the Sixty-Four Hexagrams and are explained in the forthcoming book *The Logic of the Formation of the Sixty-Four Hexagrams.*

The cardinal movements of the Before Heaven Arrangement are shown on p. 83 so that some interesting results of the different rotations can be explained. Note that the outer circle of the four configurations contain the After Heaven (AH) arrangement of trigrams with the inner circle showing the Before Heaven (BH) arrangement, which is connected to the Tai Ji Symbol.

The center images of these graphics (meaning, the hexagrams created from reading the AH trigram over the BH trigram in each graphic) are highlighted in black in each configuration. The BH trigram of Heaven is also highlighted to show its direction and placement in each of the configurations.

In Configuration 1, with the BH trigram of Heaven positioned in the South, the center of the graphic shows AH Fire over BH Heaven ䷍ (#14, *Great Possession*) and AH Water over BH Earth ䷇ (#8, *Union*) in the North.

When BH Heaven is in the position of the East (Configuration #2), the center of the graphic shows Fire over Water (#64, *Before Completion*) in the South and Water over Fire (#63, *After Completion*) in the North.

When BH Heaven is positioned in the North (Configuration #3), the center images become Fire over Earth (#35, *Advancement*) and Water over Heaven (#5, *Hesitation*).

When BH Heaven is advanced to the West (Configuration #4) the center images become Fire over Fire (#30, *Distant Brightness*) and Water over Water (#29, *The Abyss*).

The centers of all four configurations display combinations of only the images of Heaven, Earth, Fire, and Water—the four cardinal trigrams of the Before Heaven Trigram Arrangement.

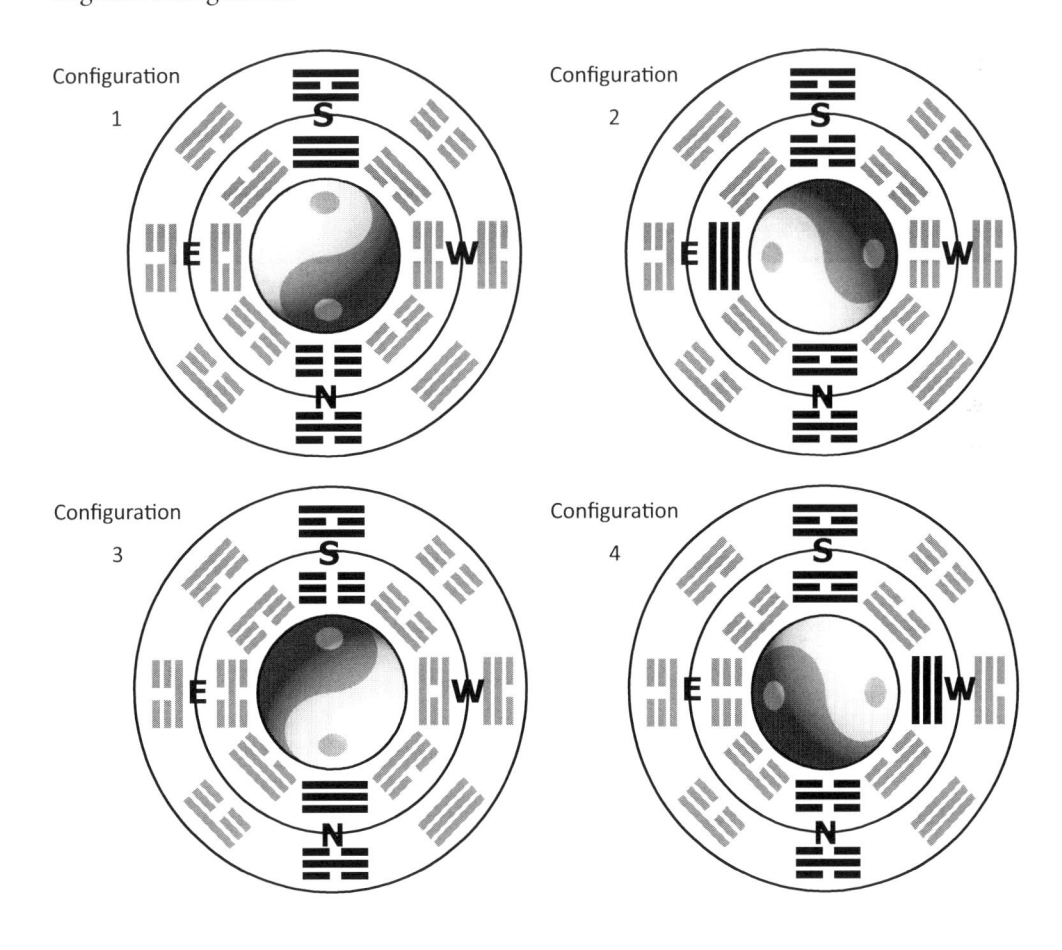

Part Seven

Using the Book of Sun and Moon

Since the *Book of Sun and Moon* is a means by which to develop and strengthen one's intuition, it is extremely important to memorize the Eight Trigrams (in both their Before Heaven and After Heaven arrangements) along with all the images and names of the Sixty-Four Hexagrams. By accomplishing this, the *Book of Sun and Moon* will become much easier to understand and use. Memory is like a muscle, and the more you exercise it the stronger and more useful it becomes. As stated earlier, imagery is one of the most powerful tools in the human psyche. Intuition is the skill of interpreting imagery and the reaction to it. For example, when driving we are constantly interpreting imagery (stop signs, road markings, yield signs, cross walks, stop and go lights, and so on). These signs (images) help us to interpret our driving and to react correctly. Imagine trying to learn to drive by only reading a book with no imagery and just written instructions. Most people would find this baffling, and extremely dangerous if they were to get behind the wheel.

The abbot and founder of the City of Ten Thousand Buddhas, Chan Master Hsuan Hua, for example, had earlier in his life performed *Yi Jing* castings for people to help raise money for his monastery. He had memorized the entire text and, consequently, was able to know the relevant hexagrams before any question was asked of him, as the imagery to him was clear from the onset. This is true mastery of the *Book of Sun and Moon*. Setting that incredible feat of memorization aside, seeking to memorize just the trigrams and hexagrams will greatly strengthen your intuition and ability to interpret the various images and help you provide a more accurate reading of a casting.

The following aspects, methods, and associations can be examined and applied to each hexagram in the *Book of Sun and Moon,* providing a wide spectrum of information to help you better interpret a hexagram casting or to examine a calculated image (such as Four Pillar and Life Path hexagrams). No matter the question put to the *Book of Sun and Moon,* they are all either asking for a divination about some future event (such as should I get married?) or trying to calculate the date, time, and/or location when to do something. So, depending on whether the question is based on divination or calculation, the information associated with each hexagram should be examined accordingly.

The Prediction and Lines

These sections contain the English translations of King Wen's *Prediction* and Duke of Zhou's *Explanation of the Lines.* My commentaries on these two sections (in *Book of Sun and Moon,* volume II) try to address what King Wen and Duke of Zhou wrote from a more Daoist perspective, rather than the Confucian interpretations that have prevailed in the past.

Commentaries on the *Yi Jing* written by Confucius and his disciples are very insightful and useful. However, the *Ten Wings* are just part of the story for learning to understand and interpret the *Yi,* and they are focused on the school of Principles of Righteousness Studies (義理學, Yi Li Xue). Several English translations on Confucian *Ten Wing's* commentaries are available, and the following three books are highly recommended:

The I Ching Book of Changes. Translated by James Legge, edited with an introduction and study guide by Ch'u Chai with Winberg Chai.

The Text of Yi King: (and Its Appendixes) Chinese Original With English Translation by Z. D. Sung.

The I Ching, or, Book of Changes by Richard Wilhelm and Cary F. Baynes.

Great Symbolism

This is the second of the *Ten Wings* attributed to Confucius. It has been included with each image in volume II of the *Book of Sun and Moon* because it not only provides valuable insights on the particular hexagram, but also shows where certain trigram correlations were developed. For example, the trigram of Wind ☴ (巽, Xun) represents both the elemental influences of "wind" and "wood." Valley ☱ (兌, Dui) is explained as either a "marsh" or "lake." Thunder ☳ (震, Zhen) is also explained as "lightning." These types of correlations were not implied or written by King Wen or Duke of Zhou, rather by Confucius.

Trigram Correlations

All the main correlations of the trigrams are given with each hexagram in volume II. The source for these correlations primarily come from the first thru eleventh chapters of the *Treatise of Remarks on the Trigrams* in the *Ten Wings* and from *A Collection on the Essentials of the Rivers He and Luo*.

In the *Book of Sun and Moon,* volume II, they are listed by subject with each hexagram. The reason for including them is that when attempting to interpret a casting, and depending on the question asked, you have immediate access to the reference material on the trigrams that comprise the particular hexagram image. For example, if a question is based on a family issue, then the trigrams of the hexagram will show the appropriate correlation with family members.

In each trigram-correlation section, the following information is provided:

Represents: lists the various assignments of the trigram.
Actions: how the trigram functions.
Influences: how the trigram interacts.
Shape: the associated shape.
Color: the associated trigram color.
Body: the associated body part.
Season: the associated trigram season.
Moon Phase: the associated Moon phase (of the eight Moon phases).
Animal: the terrestrial and celestial animals.
Directions: the Before Heaven and After Heaven directions.
Nine Palace Numbers: associated numbers from the original Fu Xi arrangement and Yu the Great's Ho River Map and Lo River Script.
Qi Center and Meridian: the associated Qi center and Nei Dan meridian.

The associated trigram Qi centers and Meridians are listed to help readers who seek to use the *Book of Sun and Moon* for determining aspects of their internal alchemy cultivation or for calculating health issues and concerns. The terms *Nei Dan* (Internal Elixir) and *Wai Dan* (External Elixir) are used to distinguish two separate systems: internal alchemy and acupuncture.

Acupuncture meridians and points can be opened and stimulated externally, whereas the internal alchemy (Nei Dan) meridians and centers can only be opened through concentrated efforts of meditative breathing and visualization exercises.

The Eight Nei Dan Qi Centers
(八內丹氣穴, **Ba Nei Dan Qi Xue**)

Heaven ☰, Muddy Pellet (泥丸, Ni Wan).

Valley ☱, Mysterious Pass (玄關, Xuan Guan).

Fire ☲, Crimson Palace (絳宮, Jiang Gong).

Thunder ☳, Elixir Field (丹田, Dan Tian).

Earth ☷, Returning Yin (回陰, Hui Yin).

Mountain ☶, Essence Gate (精門, Jing Men).

Water ☵, Double Pass (雙關, Shuang Guan).

Wind ☴, Jade Pillow (玉枕, Yu Zhen).

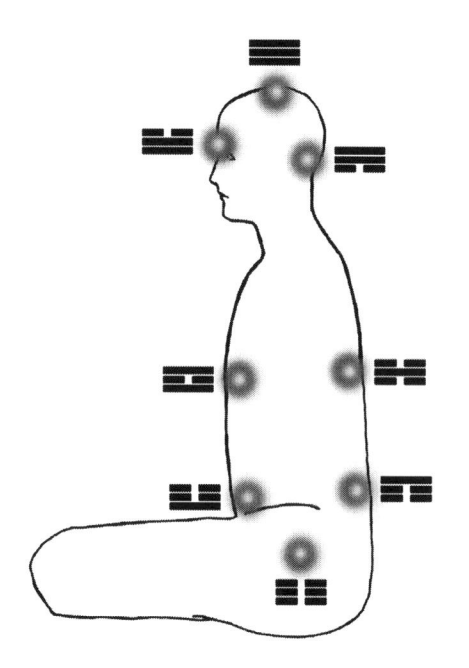

The Eight Extraordinary Nei Dan Meridians/Vessels
(內丹奇經八脈, **Nei Dan Qi Jing Ba Mai**)

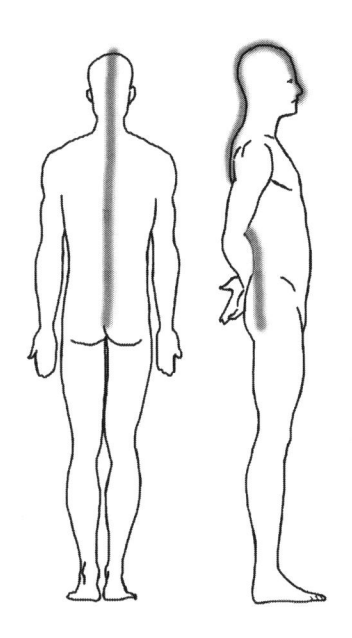

Heaven (Qian)
☰ **Control Vessel**
(督脈, Du Mai)

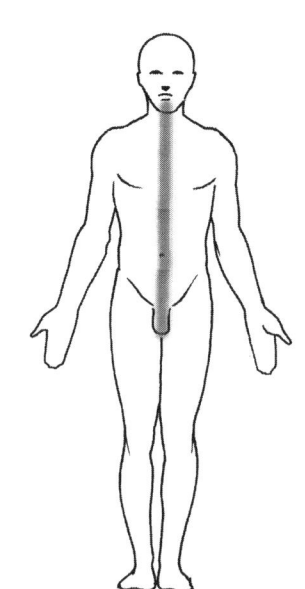

Earth (Kun)
☷ **Function Vessel**
(任脈, Ren Mai)

Fire (Li)
☲ Belt Vessel
(帶脉, Dai Mai)

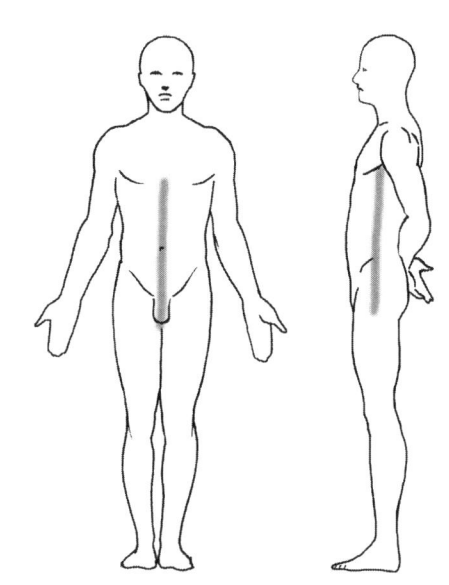

Water (Kan)
☵ Penetrating Vessel
(沖脉, Chong Mai)

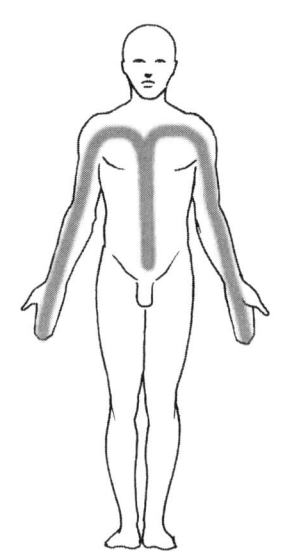

Valley (Dui)
☱ Yang Preserving Vessel
(陽維脉, Yang Wei Mai)

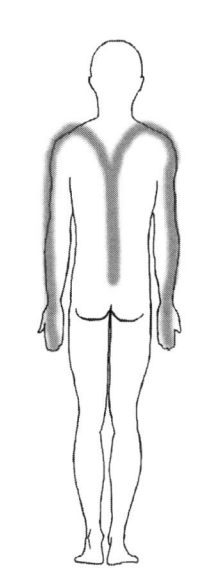

Wind (Xun)
☴ Yin Preserving Vessel
(陰維脉, Yin Wei Mai)

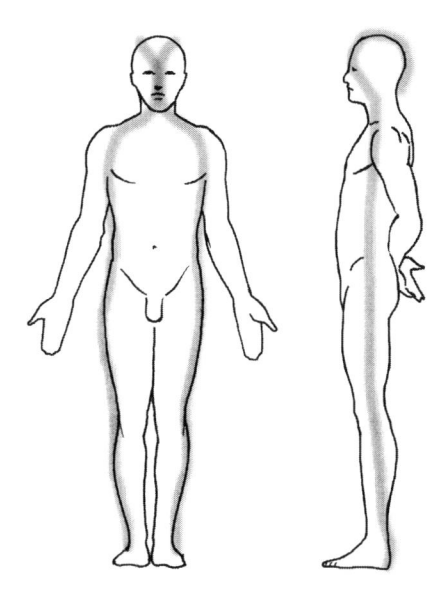

Mountain, (Gen)
⚎ Yang Heel Vessel
(陽蹻脉, Yang Qiao Mai)

Thunder, (Zhen)
⚍ Yin Heel Vessel
(陰蹻脉, Yin Qiao Mai)

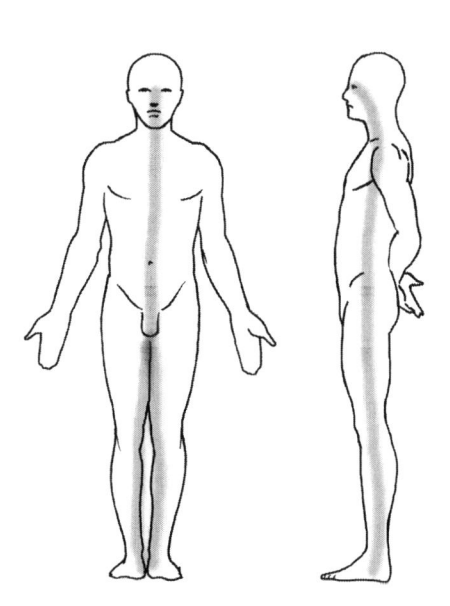

Using the Book of Sun and Moon

The Eight Wai Dan Qi Meridians (八外丹氣穴, **Ba Wai Dan Qi Xue**)

The graphic on the right comes from *A Collection on the Essentials of the Rivers He and Luo*. It shows the division of the Eight Wai Dan Qi Meridians. Translations of the Chinese in the graphic are included with the following illustrations (taken from another work)[27] which show the meridian pathways.

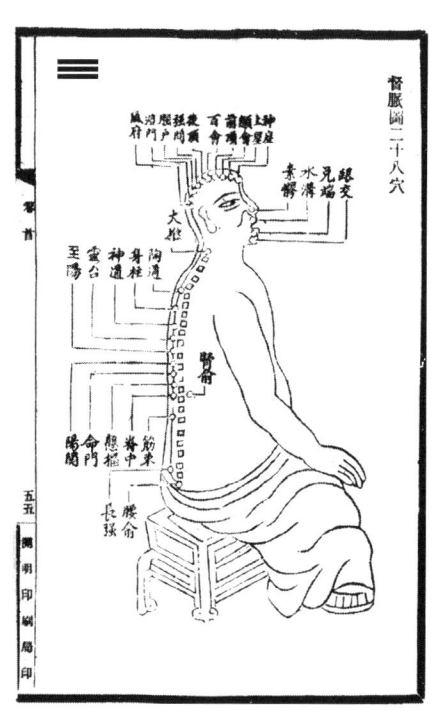

9 Heaven ☰ (乾, Qian)
Control Meridian
(督脉, Du Mai)

---

[27] These illustrations are from *Tai Ji Quan Illustrated and Explained* (太極拳圖說, *Tai Ji Quan Tu Shuo*) by Chen Pinsan and edited by Chen Panling.

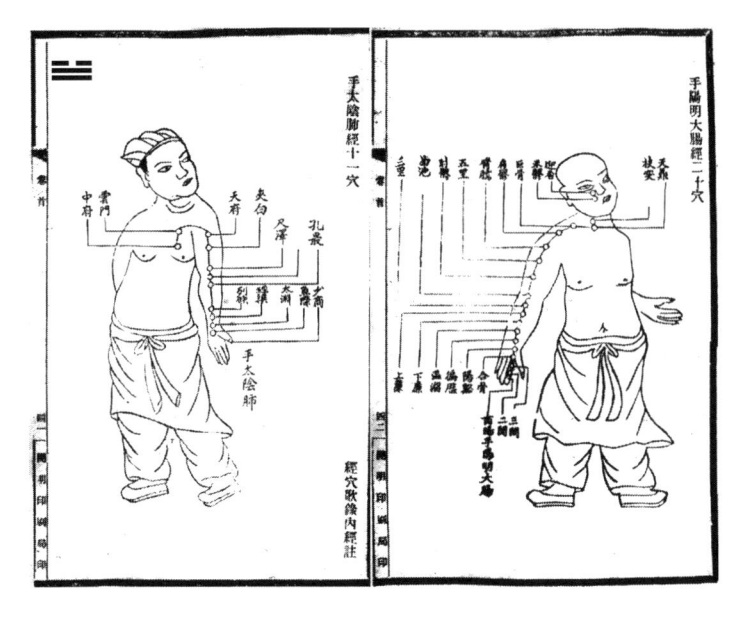

4 Valley ☱ (兌, Dui), Metal (金, Jin)

From the hands through the Ultimate Yin (太陰, Tai Yin) to affect the lungs. From the hands through Bright Yang (陽明, Yang Ming) to affect the large intestines.

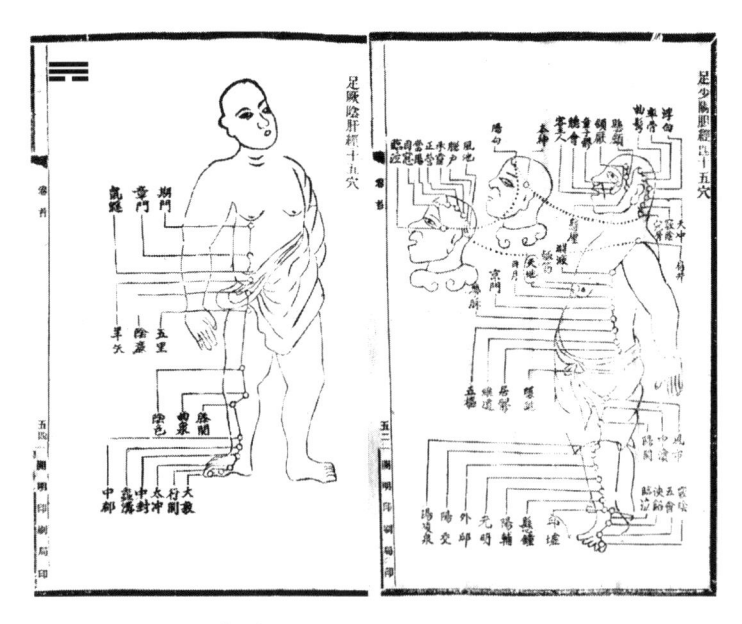

2 Wind ☴ (巽, Xun), Wood (木, Mu)

From the feet through the Young Yang to affect the gall bladder. From the Yin side of the feet (top) goes to affect the liver.

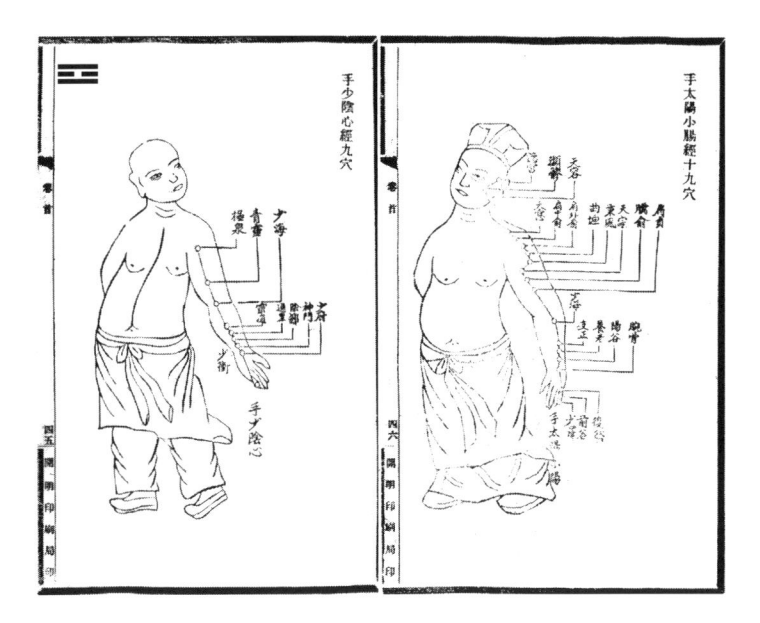

3 Fire ☲ (離, Li), Fire (火, Huo)

From the hands through Young Yin (少陰, Shao Yin) to affect the heart. From the hands through Ultimate Yang (太陽, Tai Yang) to affect the small intestines.

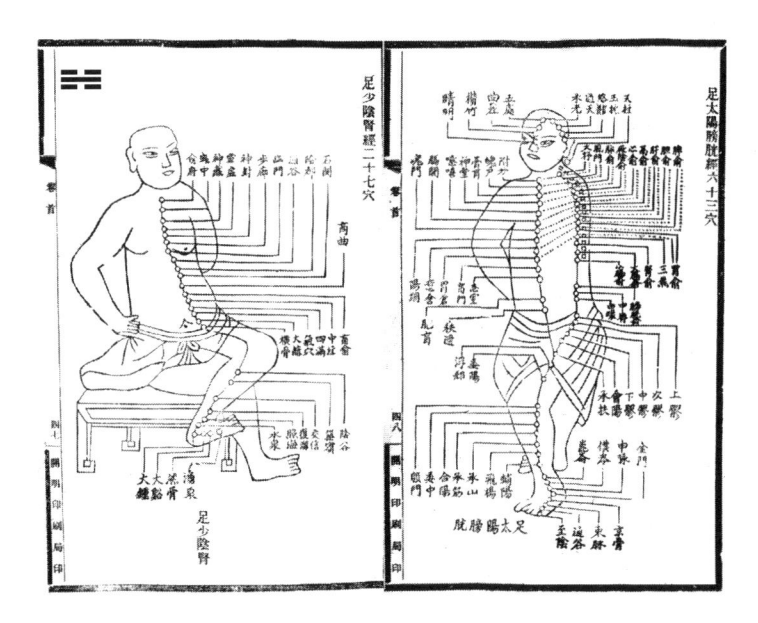

7 Water ☵ (坎, Kan), Water (水, Shui)

From the feet through Ultimate Yang to affect the bladder. From the feet through the Young Yin to affect the kidneys.

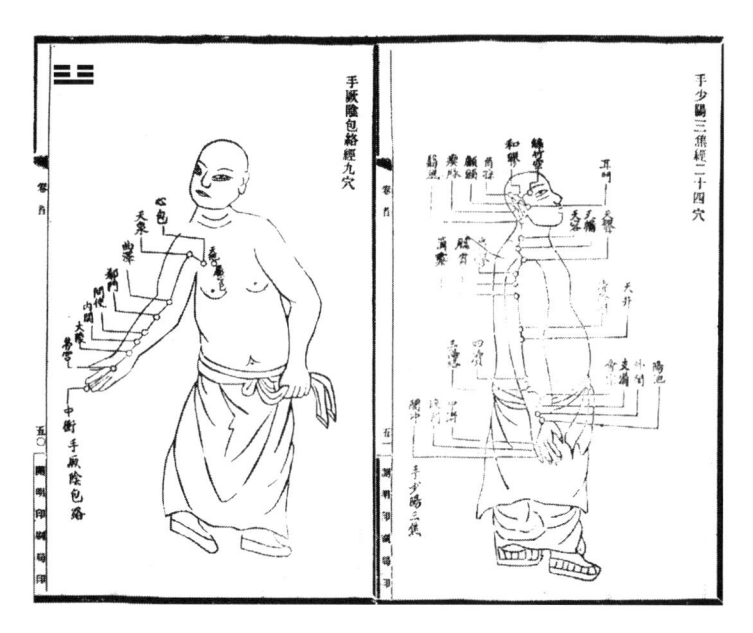

8 Thunder ☳ (震, Zhen) Thunder conjoined with Fire (相火, Xiang Huo).
From the Yin side of the hands (back) it binds around and ends in the heart. From the hands through the Young Yang (少陽, Shao Yang) to affect the Triple Warmer.

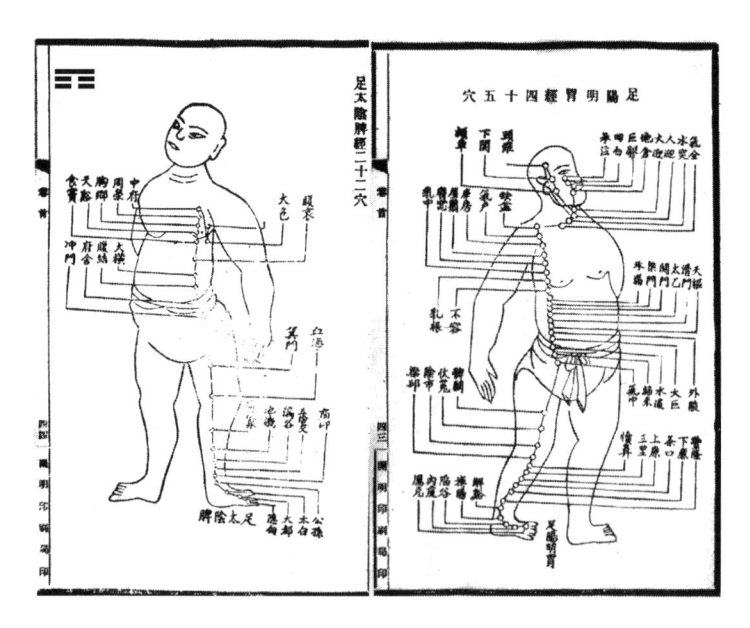

6 Mountain ☶ (艮, Gen), Earth (土, Tu)
From the feet through the Bright Yang to affect the stomach. From the feet through the Ultimate Yin to affect the spleen.

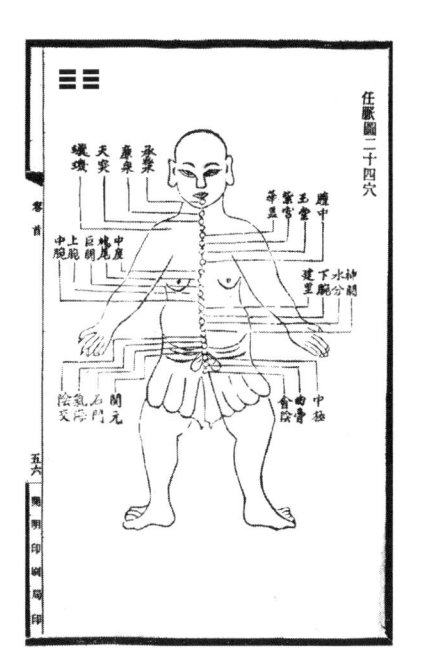

1 Earth ☷ (坤, Kun), Function Meridian (任脉, Ren Mai)

The Twenty-Eight Mansions (二十八宿, Er Shi Ba Xiu)

The very beginnings of Chinese divination, Five Element theory, and the workings of the *Book of Sun and Moon* are all predicated on cosmology. The constellations, stars, Sun, and Moon were all observed, and thus auspicious and inauspicious events could be predicted. The Ho River Map itself is a map of the Five Planets (corresponding to the Five Elements). In Daoist cosmology, the universe revolves around the Northern Bushel (北斗, Bei Dou), or Seven Star (七星, Qi Xing)—which is the Big Dipper (Ursa Major).

Daoist internal alchemy teachings correlate with these seven stars moving across the sky, with attention focused on the three stars of the handle. They associate this constellation's movements with the manner in which Qi moves around and through the Control Meridian (督脉, Du Mai) and Function Meridian (任脉, Ren Mai). Therefore, the movement of the Northern Bushel correlates with trigram and hexagram assignments. From these seven stars of the Northern Bushel, which were given the assignments of Wood, Metal, Earth, Sun, Moon, Fire, and Water, other constellations could be assigned as well.

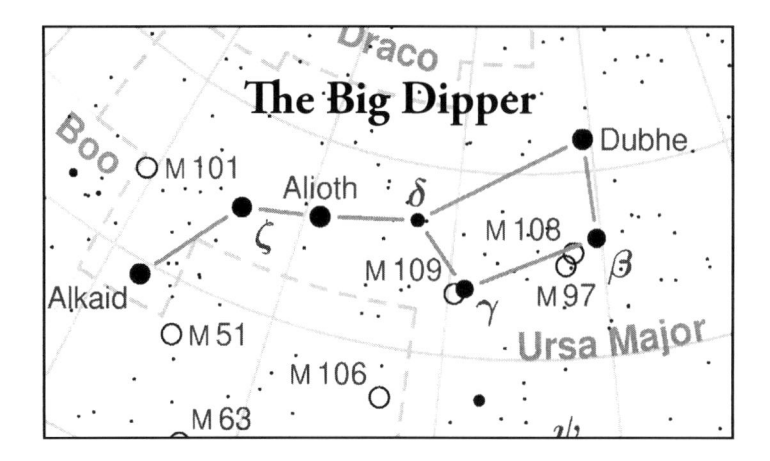

Planet and Element Correspondences of the Ho River Map

1 and 6 in the North is the Water Star (水星, Shui Xing), the planet Mercury. According to the Lunar Calendar, Mercury appears during the eleventh and sixth moons (November and June) in the early evening.

3 and 8 in the East is the Wood Star (木星, Mu Xing), the planet Jupiter. It appears in the third and eighth moons (March and August) in the early evening.

2 and 7 in the South is the Fire Star (火星, Huo Xing), the planet Mars. It appears in the second and seventh moons (February and July) in the early evening.

5 and 10 in the Center is the Earth Star (土星, Tu Xing), the planet Saturn. It appears in the middle of the sky during the fifth and tenth moons (May and October) in the early evening.

4 and 9 in the West is the Metal Star (金星, Jin Xing), the planet Venus. It appears during the fourth and ninth moons (April and September) in the early evening.

Using the Book of Sun and Moon

The Twenty-Eight Constellations

The Twenty-Eight Constellations are divided into four divisions with seven constellations (mansions) indicated within them. The Four Quadrants include:

Green Dragon (青龍, Qing Long) in the East (Fire ☲).

Black Turtle (玄武, Xuan Wu) in the North (Earth ☷).

White Tiger (白虎, Bai Hu) in the West (Water ☵).

Vermillion Bird (朱雀, Zhu Que) in the South (Heaven ☰).

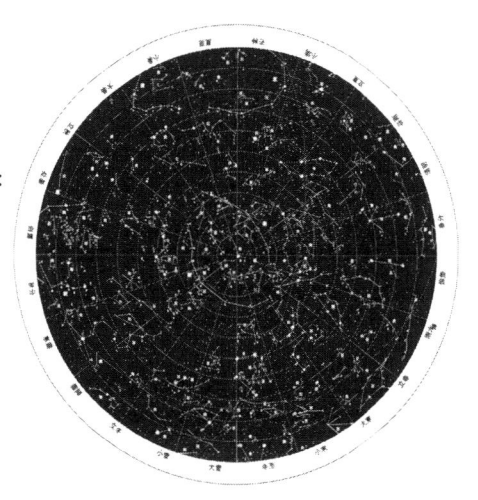

The Four Quadrants with Associated After Heaven Houses

97

The Seven Mansions of the Twenty-Eight Constellations

The Seven Mansions in the Eastern Sky, Green Dragon, Spring
3 and 8, Jupiter

It takes approximately twelve years for Jupiter to orbit the Sun and align with Earth (according to the Lunar Calendar).

3, After Heaven House of Thunder, ☳ *Arousing Movement*
8, After Heaven House of Mountain, ☶ *Determined Stillness*

Constellations

1) Horn (角, Jiao)	Wood	Spica
2) Neck (亢, Kang)	Metal	Virgo
3) Root (氐, Di)	Earth	Libra
4) Room (房, Fang)	Sun	Libra
5) Heart (心, Xin)	Moon	Antares
6) Tail (尾, Wei)	Fire	Scorpio
7) Basket (箕, Ji)	Water	Sagittarius

The Seven Mansions of the Northern Sky, Black Turtle, Winter
1 and 6, Mercury

It takes approximately four months for Mercury to orbit the Sun and align with the Earth (according to the Lunar Calendar).

1, After Heaven House of Water, ☵ *The Abyss*
6, After Heaven House of Heaven, ☰ *Creativity of Heaven*

Constellations

8) Dipper (斗, Dou)	Wood	Sagittarius
9) Ox (牛, Niu)	Metal	Capricorn
10) Girl (女, Nu)	Earth	Aquarius
11) Emptiness (虛, Xu)	Sun	Aquarius Equuleus
12) Roof (危, Wei)	Moon	Aquarius Pegasus
13) Chamber (室, Shi)	Fire	Pegasus
14) Wall (壁, Bi)	Water	Pegasus

The Seven Mansions of the Western Sky, White Tiger, Autumn

4 and 9, Venus

It takes Venus approximately eight months to orbit the Sun and align with Earth (according to the Lunar Calendar).

    4, After Heaven House of Wind, ☴ *Submission*

    9, After Heaven House of Fire, ☲ *Distant Brightness*

Constellations

15) Legs (奎, Kui)	Wood	Andromeda Pisces
16) Bond (婁, Lou)	Metal	Aries
17) Stomach (胃, Wei)	Earth	Musca Borealis
18) Head Hair (昴, Mao)	Sun	Pleiades
19) Net (畢, Bi)	Moon	Taurus
20) Turtle Beak (觜, Zi)	Fire	Orion
21) Three Stars (參, Shen)	Water	Orion

The Seven Mansions of the Southern Sky, Vermillion Bird, Summer

2 and 7, Mars

It takes Mars approximately two years to orbit the sun and align with Earth (according to the Lunar Calendar).

    2, After Heaven House of Earth, ☷ *Receptivity of Earth*

    7, After Heaven House of Valley, ☱ *Joyousness*

Constellations

22) Well (井, Jing)	Wood	Gemini
23) Ghost (鬼, Gui)	Metal	Cancer
24) Willow (柳, Liu)	Earth	Hydra
25) Star (星, Xing)	Sun	Alphard
26) Long Net (張, Zhang)	Moon	Crater
27) Wings (翼, Yi)	Fire	Corvus
28) Chariot (軫, Zhen)	Water	Corvus

Center of the Sky, Northern Bushel

Visible throughout the year (in the northern hemisphere).

5 and 10, Saturn

It takes Saturn approximately twenty-eight years to orbit the Sun and align with the Earth (according to the Lunar Calendar).

The charts and explanations of the Twenty-Eight Mansions show that the Ho River Map and Lo River Script were initially diagrams of cosmological occurrences. The Ho River Map, for example, reveals an unfolding into the Lo River Script. Although much more information exists on Chinese cosmology, this was just a basic summary of how the *Book of Sun and Moon* and cosmology relate to each other, and of their early development in Chinese culture.

Associated Developed Hexagrams From Casting

Whenever an image is cast, six associated hexagrams are automatically created as well. From the Before Heaven Hexagram (the casted image), the following hexagrams develop: 1) Contrasted Image Hexagram, 2) Eight Gates Hexagram, 3) After Heaven Hexagram, 4) Sun, Moon, or Eclipse Hexagram, 5) Ruling Line Hexagram, and 6) Inner Image Hexagram—as well as any possible Changing Line Hexagram(s).

These six hexagrams (and any possible Changing Line image) represent the situation at the time of casting the Before Heaven Hexagram. Together, they act like the footprints a tracker would follow or the clues a detective would investigate to provide the answers and relevant information about a given question or situation.

In the *Book of Sun and Moon,* volume II, the six associated hexagrams for each of the Sixty-Four Hexagrams are shown for easy calculation. These hexagrams can be grouped into two sets of four hexagrams: The first set includes the Before Heaven, Contrasted Image, Eight Gates, and After Heaven images, and the second set of four hexagrams includes the Before Heaven image (again), with its corresponding Sun, Moon, or Eclipse Hexagram, the Ruling Line Hexagram, and the Inner Image Hexagram.

These groups of hexagrams can be viewed and examined as if employing a triangulation process to pinpoint the end trail of a situation or event. In analogy (for the first four hexagrams), this is like a detective or tracker seeing and following footprints or clues, and then clarifying the clues to find the person or destination of the tracks. The second set of four hexagrams, then, is like the tracker or detective determining the purpose or intent behind the person's movements or why the situation headed in the direction it did—so the second set of hexagrams can be seen as an interrogation of the person or examination of the situation's result.

In simpler terms, the first four hexagrams can be called "The Seen" or "Visible Hexagrams," and the second four, "The Unseen" or "Invisible Hexagrams." Hence, the Before Heaven Hexagram in conjunction with the Contrasted Image, Eight Gates, and After Heaven hexagrams are almost entirely about examining the visible clues and tracks. Whereas, the Before Heaven Hexagram in conjunction with the Sun, Moon, or Eclipse Hexagram, the Ruling Line Hexagram, and the Inner Image Hexagram represent what is not visible or apparent in the situation. If these hexagrams were to be placed in a circle, like the arrangements of the Eight Trigrams, the first four hexagrams would be positioned on the Yang side, and the second four on the Yin side, with the Before Heaven Hexagram occupying both the North and South positions.

First Triangulation (The Seen)

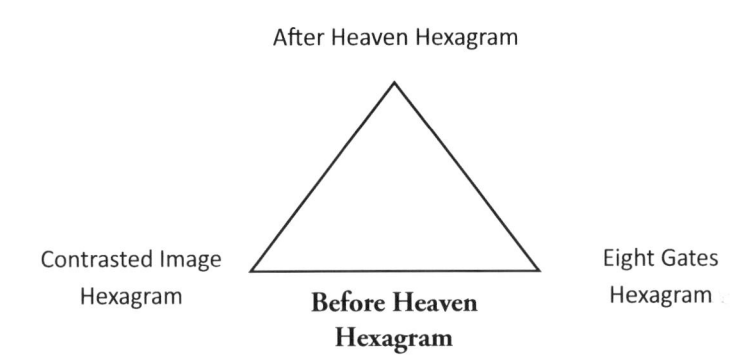

```
                After Heaven Hexagram
                         △
Contrasted Image                      Eight Gates
   Hexagram        Before Heaven       Hexagram
                     Hexagram
```

Before Heaven Hexagram (先天卦)

This image, the original casted hexagram, is revealing the foundation of the situation. The movements of each individual line, the interaction of the upper and lower trigrams, and the hexagram itself are showing the overall view of the situation. By its Before Heaven nature, this image, in essence, is unchanging and fixed, and therefore forms the basis for all the following and correlated hexagrams. Using the analogy of a tracker, this hexagram is like finding a footprint and then discerning certain facts about the size of the person or animal, speed of movement, state of health or injury, and so on.

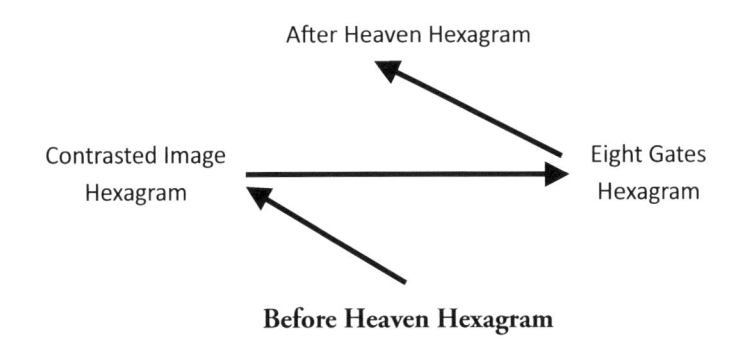

```
                After Heaven Hexagram
                         ↖
Contrasted Image     ───────────→     Eight Gates
   Hexagram            ↖               Hexagram

                Before Heaven Hexagram
```

Contrasted Image Hexagram (對卦)

This hexagram is the exact opposite of the casted Before Heaven image. All things, whether real, imagined, or yet to exist, have an opposing view, situation, or condition, so the Contrasted Image Hexagram indicates where the situation could head if the oracle is not followed. For example, if hexagram #11 ䷊, *Peacefulness,* were cast, its opposite image would be #12 ䷋, *Adversity.* Therefore, if not following the advice for *Peacefulness,* the influences of *Adversity* will result.

The Contrasted Image Hexagram, moreover, serves as an indication of the Yin and Yang balance of the Before Heaven Hexagram. This is not unlike the tracker who discovers a footprint, but then needs to find the opposite footprint to determine the stride, weight, or any anomalies in the person's or animal's movements or body.

Eight Gates Hexagram (八門卦)

This hexagram reveals the connection between the Contrasted Image Hexagram and the After Heaven Hexagram. For instance, looking at the example above with #11 ䷊, *Peacefulness,* possibly turning to #12 ䷋, *Adversity,* the connection for that would be hexagram #64 ䷿, *Before Completion,* the Eight Gates image. This illustrates the idea that *Adversity* could come into play because the tenants of *Peacefulness* were not followed correctly, and so the effects of *Before Completion* cause *Adversity*. In the analogy of a tracker, the Eight Gates Hexagram is like revealing the direction in which the footprints are heading and why they are heading that way.

After Heaven Hexagram (後天卦)

This hexagram shows what the successful or unsuccessful conclusion of the situation could be depending on the casted Before Heaven Hexagram. In other words, the After Heaven Hexagram is a reflection of the outcome or function of the situation in the Before Heaven Hexagram.

Again, if hexagram #11 ䷊, *Peacefulness,* resulted from a casting, the After Heaven Hexagram would be #63 ䷾, *After Completion.* This would show, for example, that *Peacefulness* (the image of meditation) could lead to the conditions of attaining immortality. Hence, these two hexagrams express the idea of a successful conclusion.

In the case of a casted hexagram being #12 ䷋, *Adversity,* the After Heaven Hexagram would be #64 ䷿, *Before Completion,* expressing the idea that the situation is, or will be, unsuccessful.

In the analogy of the tracker, the After Heaven Hexagram is very much like the tracker finally seeing the person or animal being tracked.

Second Triangulation (The Unseen)

Before Heaven Hexagram

Sun/Moon/Eclipse Hexagram — Ruling Line Hexagram

Inner Image Hexagram

The **Before Heaven Hexagram** is again the foundational hexagram for determining the second triangulation.

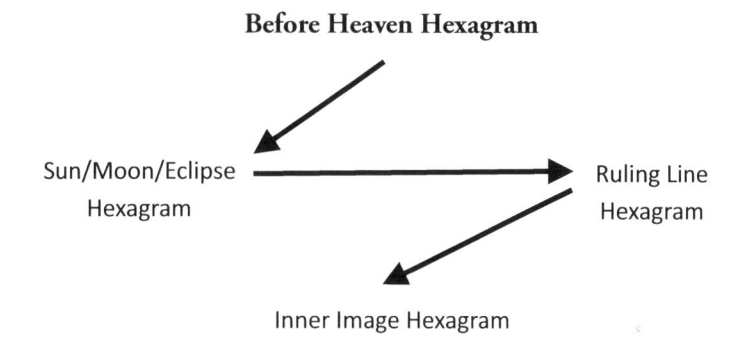

Before Heaven Hexagram

Sun/Moon/Eclipse Hexagram → Ruling Line Hexagram

Inner Image Hexagram

Sun or Moon Hexagram (日月卦)

The Sun or Moon image is determined by the Before Heaven Hexagram and shows the natural progression of the external situation and the natural course of change in the sequence of the hexagrams in the *Book of Sun and Moon*. For example, if you cast the Before Heaven Hexagram #3, *Beginning Difficulties,* hexagram #4, *Untaught Youth,* will automatically become its Moon image. Conversely, if the Before Heaven Hexagram #4, *Untaught Youth,* were cast, then hexagram #3, *Beginning Difficulties,* will automatically become its Sun image, the natural direction in which the situation is heading. Depending on the Before Heaven Hexagram cast, the Sun or Moon Hexagram could bring good fortune or misfortune. Sun hexagrams (because they are Yang) tend towards predicting good fortune, and Moon hexagrams (because they are Yin) tend towards predicting misfortune.

To the tracker, a Sun Hexagram reveals more clarity about a person or situation (like tracking in the daylight), while a Moon Hexagram tends to show the darker or more concealed aspects of the person or situation.

Eclipse Hexagram (食卦)

Within the *Book of Sun and Moon,* four specific hexagrams correlate with Lunar Eclipses (月食, Yue Shi) and Solar Eclipses (日食, Ri Shi). These are #27 and #28 in the *Upper Book,* and #61 and #62 in the *Lower Book.*

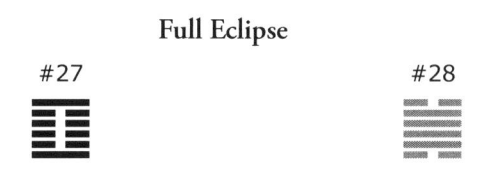

Full Eclipse

#27   #28

Image #27 shows the Moon eclipsing the Sun. Lines one and six show the light of the Sun being diminished, and completely obscured in lines two through five. Image #28 shows the Sun blocking the light of the Moon, likewise fully eclipsing lines two through five.

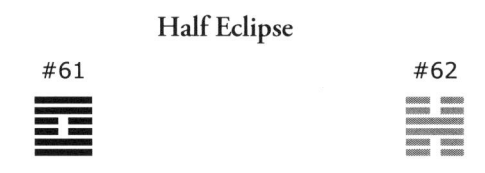

Half Eclipse

#61   #62

In image #61, a partial Lunar Eclipse is blocking the Sun, seen in lines three and four. A partial Solar Eclipse is blocking the light of the Moon in image #62, also revealed in lines three and four.

In early Chinese folklore, eclipses were considered to be omens of misfortune, foretelling of a coming disaster, and, like comets, seen as a sign of a powerful demon entering or being born into the world. In the case of the above hexagrams, #27 shows Thunder within a Mountain, an image of a pending volcanic eruption and earthquake. Valley over Wind, in image #28, shows a strong movement beneath water, such as a tsunami. Image #61, Wind over Valley, shows the effects of tidal waves from a tsunami, and #62, Thunder over Mountain, shows the effects of a volcanic eruption (the mountain top being blown off). Hence, if one of these Eclipse Hexagrams is cast as a Before Heaven image, consider the influences that the short-term, yet powerful, aspects built into these images can have on the situation.

Ruling Line Hexagram (君爻卦)

The Ruling Line Hexagram tends to reveal the more hidden aspects of the person or situation. In other words, the more latent qualities. Since Ruling Lines are indications of the power centers of a hexagram they should be viewed as the personality of the person or situation, and it is always best, like a Changing Line Hexagram, to read the text of the Ruling Line in the Before Heaven Hexagram and the corresponding line in the Ruling Line Hexagram. To the detective, this hexagram is very much like discovering the personality type of the person being interrogated, and because this hexagram reveals such traits, examining the hexagram's corresponding Chinese animal astrological sign (see the Sixty-Year Cycle of Hexagrams Chart on p. 77) will provide even deeper insights.

Inner Image Hexagram (內卦)
The Inner Image Hexagram reveals the very core and root conditions of the person or situation at hand. The Inner Image Hexagram should never be determined by changing lines. Always calculate the Inner Image Hexagram from the original Before Heaven Hexagram. The bottom trigram is created by taking the second, third, and fourth lines of the Before Heaven Hexagram. The upper trigram is created by taking the third, fourth, and fifth lines of the Before Heaven Hexagram. These two trigrams then form the Inner Image Hexagram.

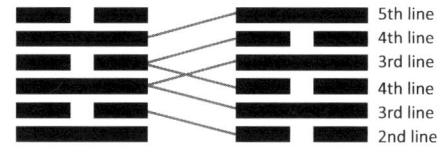

In the analogy of the detective and tracker, the underlying motivations for why a person committed a crime or fled to a certain direction is as equally important as examining their current movements and where the situation is heading. The Inner Image Hexagram, then, goes to the heart of what is being generated and expressed by the person or situation concerning the question being asked of the *Book of Sun and Moon*. Meaning, it is as important to examine the motives behind why a question is being asked, rather than the actual answer to the question.

Triangulation of Hexagrams
In comparing "The Seen" and "The Unseen" triangulated sets of hexagrams, certain relationships reveal themselves. For example, the Contrasted Image Hexagram relates to the Sun/Moon/Eclipse Hexagram, the Eight Gates Hexagram relates to the Ruling Line Hexagram, and the After Heaven Hexagram relates to the Inner Image Hexagram. Note, however, that space for a Changing Line Hexagram is not

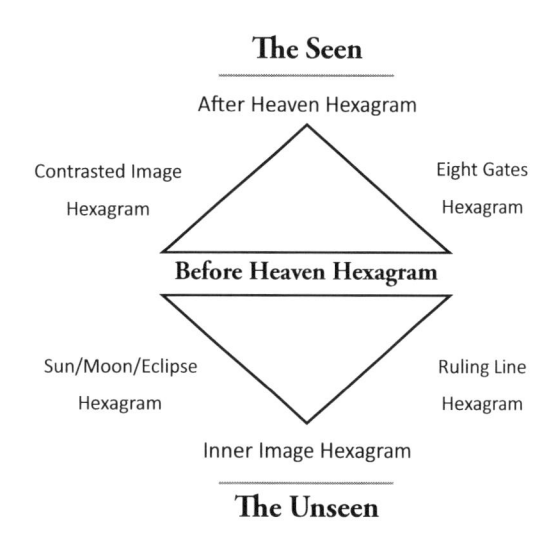

105

shown. This is because a Changing Line Hexagram would create a whole new pattern of triangulation with its own set of six associated hexagrams.

Examples of Traditional Methods of Triangulation

Regarding the subject of triangulation within the *Book of Sun and Moon*, this aspect for calculation has been widely used by Chinese astrologers, divinators, and calculators since ancient times. In Chinese astrology it is used to determine even the most basic of correlations, such as determining the two compatible animals for any given animal sign. For example, when looking at the wheel showing the Twelve Animals, the most compatible associations for any given animal sign sit four positions to the right of the given animal and four to the left, making a triangulated relationship. For example, Rat is compatible with Monkey and Dragon—this is what can be classified as *The Seen*. The Rat, however, is not compatible with Horse (its opposite sign) nor the Dog or Tiger—of which their triangulation can be called *The Unseen*. These triangulations can be constructed with each of the Twelve Animals in the Chinese Zodiac.

The Seen ▬▬▬▬

    Rat's most favorable signs are Dragon and Monkey.

The Unseen ▬ ▬ ▬ ▬

    Rat's least favorable signs are Horse, Dog, and Tiger.

Using the Book of Sun and Moon

The center of this traditional diagram[28] displays the Four Celestial Animals (Green Dragon, Black Turtle, White Tiger, and Vermillion Bird) associated with the Twenty-Eight Constellations. The next circle shows the After Heaven Eight Trigrams, while the third circle shows the Twelve Astrological Animals. The outer circle of Chinese lists the Twelve Earthly Branches, Ten Heavenly Stems, and the After Heaven positions of Heaven (乾, Qian) and Earth (坤, Kun).

The Four Celestial Animals, Eight Trigrams, and Twelve Animal Signs create the twenty-four divisions that are then used to determine the twenty-four seasons of a year (each month is divided into Yin and Yang periods), the twelve Chinese hours in a day (also divided into Yin and Yang periods, making twenty-four time periods in a day).

Note that each of the eight divisions (shown more clearly in the illustration on p. 106) contains three indicators (using the Twelve Earthly Branches and Ten Heavenly Stems) for showing the correlations with the Eight Trigrams—a method of triangulation for determining associations with all the elements in the diagram.

---

[28] Illustration is from *Chinese Horoscopes: The Twelve Signs and What They Mean* by Catherine Aubier (Crescent Books, 1988).

Beyond the correlation of triangulation within Chinese astrology this method was used even within the Nine Palaces and later correlated with the Eight Trigrams, thus becoming part of how the Sixty-Four Hexagrams could be used in calculation. These correlations then could be used to determine not only the years, but the month, day, hour, and minutes as well. In the book *A Collection on the Essentials of the Rivers He and Luo,* the following series of diagrams show a variety of examples of triangulation.

Diagram One, titled *An Illustration of the He River Map Embodying the Eight Trigrams, Five Elements, and Ten Heavenly Stems,* shows how these three systems of calculation work together in triangulation.

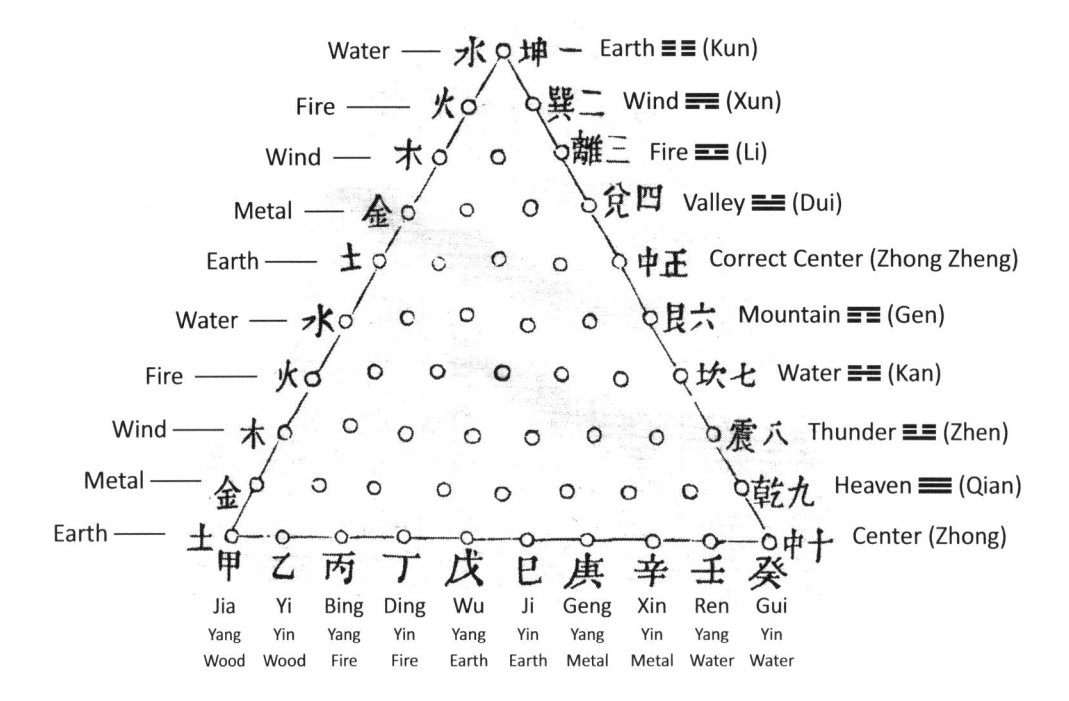

```
           Water ── 水○ 坤一 ── Earth ☷ (Kun)
            Fire ── 火○  ○巽二 Wind ☴ (Xun)
            Wind ── 木○  ○ ○離三 Fire ☲ (Li)
           Metal ── 金○ ○ ○ ○兑四 Valley ☱ (Dui)
           Earth ── 土○ ○ ○ ○ ○中正 Correct Center (Zhong Zheng)
           Water ── 水○ ○ ○ ○ ○ ○艮六 Mountain ☶ (Gen)
            Fire ── 火○ ○ ○ ○ ○ ○ ○坎七 Water ☵ (Kan)
            Wind ── 木○ ○ ○ ○ ○ ○ ○ ○震八 Thunder ☳ (Zhen)
           Metal ── 金○ ○ ○ ○ ○ ○ ○ ○ ○乾九 Heaven ☰ (Qian)
           Earth ── 土○─○─○─○─○─○─○─○─○─○中十 Center (Zhong)
                     甲  乙  丙  丁  戊  巳  庚  辛  壬  癸
                     Jia Yi Bing Ding Wu  Ji Geng Xin Ren Gui
                    Yang Yin Yang Yin Yang Yin Yang Yin Yang Yin
                    Wood Wood Fire Fire Earth Earth Metal Metal Water Water
```

108

Diagram Two is titled *The Six Zi Responding With the Six Qi*. The *Six Zi* is a reference to Zi (子) the first of the Twelve Earthly Branches. Throughout the Sixty-Year Cycle it appears six times, thus "Six Zi." The *Six Qi*, a reference to the six lines in a hexagram, are the climate influences of Yin and Yang (cold, heat, drought, moisture, wind, and fire), and this process of correlating them can be extended to each of the other eleven branches. The Six Qi is also referring to Yin and Yang (in their unchanging modes) of wind, rain, darkness, and light. Triangulation measures were also used in conjunction with the Eight Trigrams to determine these correlations. In this diagram, the Eight Trigrams are in the Before Heaven Arrangement.

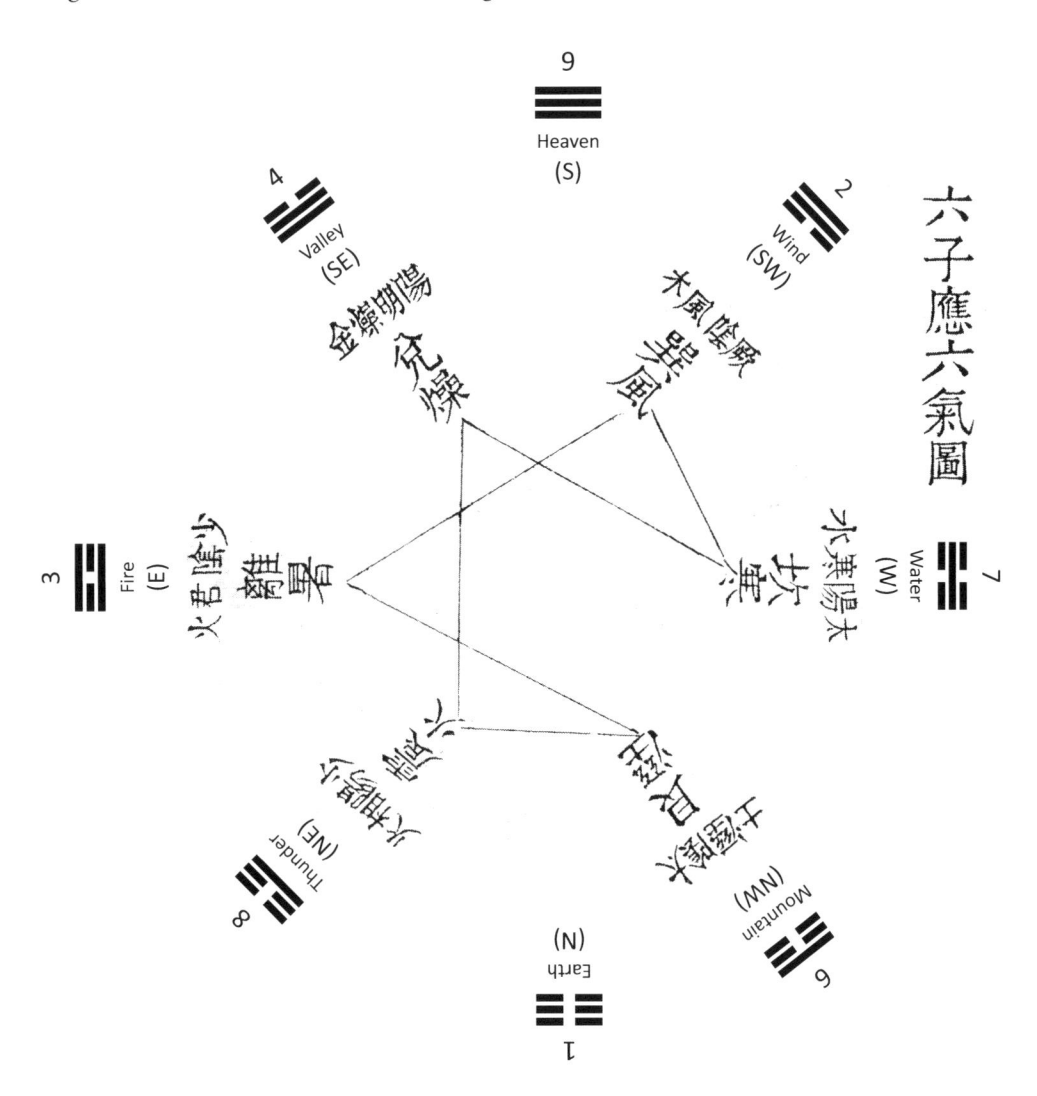

Book of Sun and Moon

Diagram Three is titled *An Illustration of the Level and Circular Divisions for Obtaining Numerological Numbering*. In this diagram, the Ten Heavenly Stems are being used as the indicators of position but could equally expand out to the Twelve Earthly Branches, Eight Trigrams, Nine Palaces, Sixty-Four Hexagrams, and so on. This diagram is a rudimentary exhibit of how triangulation can be determined in both a macro and micro calculation.

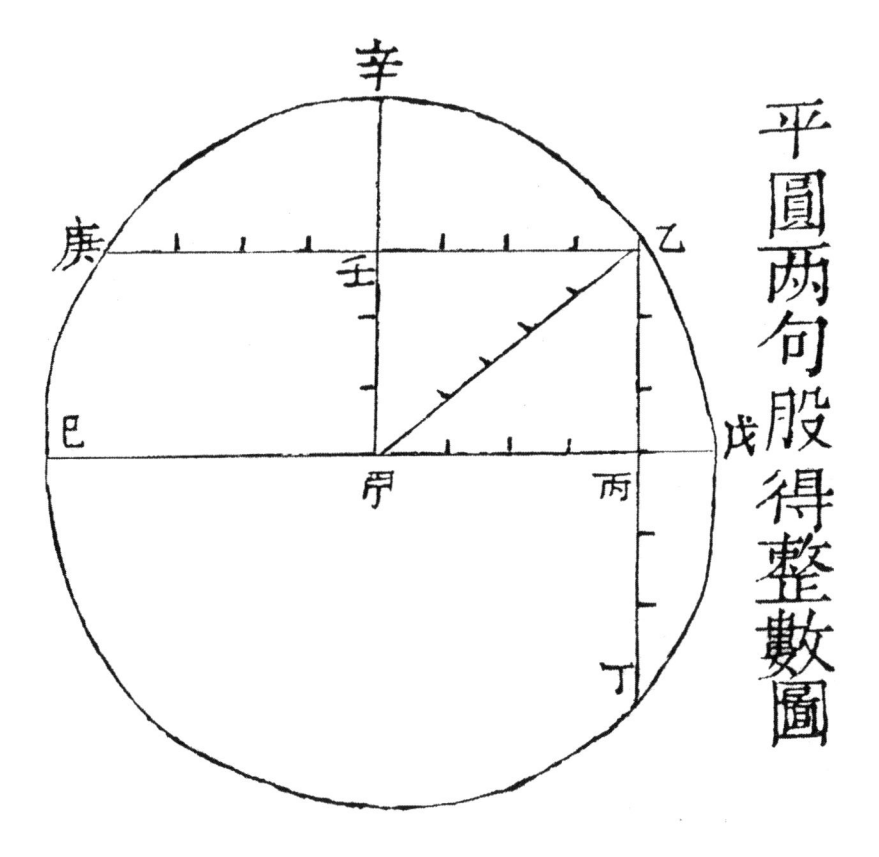

110

Combining Diagrams Four, Five, Six, and Seven shows how the four quadrants (see page 97, the Twenty-Eight Constellations) were determined by triangulation. Again, this process can be used for various other means and calculations.

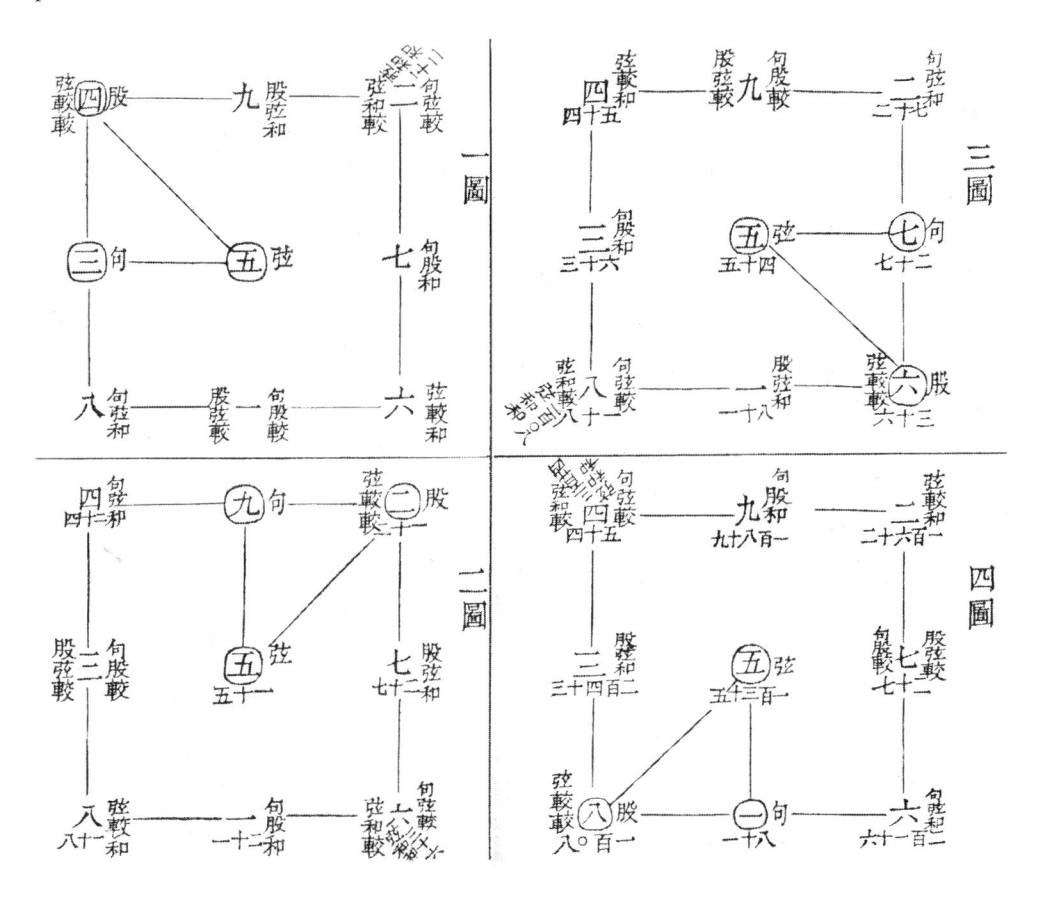

All these examples show how triangulation has been used throughout the traditional methods of divination and calculation for the *Book of Sun and Moon*. How far back this method goes into Chinese culture is unknown, but most likely it began during the time of Yu the Great and his creation of the Nine Palaces. In the *Book of Sun and Moon*, volume II, each hexagram includes the triangulation of *The Seen* and *The Unseen* Associated Developed Hexagrams (see p. 114 for an example), making it far easier for the reader to reference them. For some reason, this aspect of calculation is rarely explained in the multitude of books published on the *Book of Changes,* and even in most books on Feng Shui. This is surprising because it has, since ancient times, been a foundational method for calculating. Hopefully, by presenting it in these volumes of the *Book of Sun and Moon* there will be a renewed interest in this subject of triangulation.

Example for Interpreting a Casted Before Heaven Hexagram

Let's assume a random question was put to the *Book of Sun and Moon,* such as "Should Betty seek a new career?" After manipulating the stalks, the Before Heaven Hexagram results as #15 *Modesty.* This hexagram creates the Associated Hexagrams of #10 *Treading* (Contrasted Image Hexagram), #50 *The Cauldron* (Eight Gates), #5 *Hesitation* (After Heaven), #16 *Joyful Ease* (Moon), #2 *Receptivity of Earth* (Ruling Line), and #40 *Liberation* (Inner Image Hexagram). The following brief outline shows how these Associated Hexagrams affect the interpretations of the casting.

See *Book of Sun and Moon,* volume II, for further information on each hexagram as well as their Associated Developed Hexagrams.

First Triangulation (The Seen)

#15 *Modesty*

Modesty shows a Mountain within the Earth, which reveals Betty's strength of conviction. She should first consider what her strengths and weaknesses are, and then bring balance to both. In other words, she needs to decide what her strongest interests and desires are in connection with her livelihood.

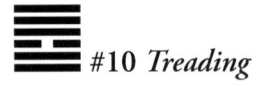

#10 *Treading*

The Contrasted Image Hexagram of *Treading* shows there must be clear thinking and caution before embarking on seeking a new career. Treading carefully so as not to step on the tiger's tail.

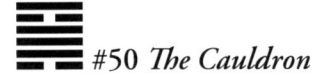

#50 *The Cauldron*

The Eight Gates Hexagram is *The Cauldron,* showing that if she wants to change careers, it is best to seek out employment connected to her innermost desire (what she feels is her destiny, or to act on her dreams); otherwise, there will be unhappiness. The Cauldron shows a change in perception, and the change is about the willingness to sacrifice.

#5 *Hesitation*

The After Heaven Hexagram is *Hesitation,* which shows that her patience, clear thinking, preparation, and modesty are rewarded. A celebration is predicted (eating and drinking joyfully) indicating she will achieve success in her endeavor.

Second Triangulation (The Unseen)

#15 *Modesty*

Betty's strength comes from a yearning to get out of her present situation, but her weakness has always been falling back on the support and issues of pleasing her mother. This is something she keeps secret from others—going between true modesty and false modesty.

#16 *Joyful Ease*

The Moon Hexagram is *Joyful Ease,* showing Thunder within the Earth. Her seeking a new career will agitate her mother, so she must bring peace to the situation. To achieve *Joyful Ease,* She needs to make offerings to her mother to appease her and gain her support.

#2 *Receptivity of Earth*

The Ruling Line Hexagram is *Receptivity of Earth*. The third Ruling Line of *Modesty* says, "A wise person of Modesty and merit. Auspiciousness exists to the end." The third line of *Receptivity of Earth* reads, "Restrained excellence through being resolute. Complying with the king's affairs is without success in the end." These lines show that if Betty's modesty is true and comes from wisdom, good fortune will follow. This is similar to the Biblical verse, "The meek shall inherit the Earth." But in this case it is more like, "The modest inherits good fortune." So in Betty's endeavor to seek a new career she must be restrained about showing off her excellence, because to do otherwise is not true modesty. The third line here also indicates she would probably be better off to seek out starting her own business, as complying with the dictates of a boss (the king) will not bring success.

#40 *Liberation*

The Inner Image Hexagram is *Liberation* and this shows Thunder rising out of the Water. Water is symbolic of wealth, and Thunder shows the stimulation of it. In Betty's case, according to *The Prediction* of *Liberation,* she must seek out the Southwest, and Southwest here signifies Wind and Earth, the Before and After Heaven trigrams that occupy the position of the Southwest. These trigrams show that the mother (Earth) must be moved (Wind) from her present stance and opinions of Betty starting her own business, along with her mother's support (financial to be precise). So it is like not going anywhere, yet returning to where she should be. "Having somewhere to go," means Betty needs to change her position and view on her means of livelihood, and to be successful, she must begin to work early in the morning to show her sincerity and diligence.

Summary

Betty needs to first stand up to her mother and show sincerity in her endeavor to change her career, and be resolute about it. She must demonstrate to her mother how much better their lives will be with this change. She needs to plan out her new endeavor carefully and with patience, and to clearly look at her flaws and her strengths in business so to bring balance to her plan. From this she can gain the emotional and financial support of her mother. All the hexagrams show success in Betty seeking a new career, which should be based on improving people's and worker's rights through the law.

This casting shows this career path because *Modesty* indicates supporting equality. *Treading* indicates agitating the powers that be (the tiger's tail) to aid in the will of the people. *The Cauldron* indicates the idea of sacrifice and healing. *Hesitation* indicates the display of boldness to incite debate from the opposition. *Joyful Ease* shows a group of competent people (princes) coming together to form a coalition (army) to battle inequality (from the idea of *Modesty*). *Receptivity of Earth* is about being generous and providing support to people and things in a weaker position. Finally, *Liberation* indicates a releasing and change of laws that create unjust penalties and punishments.

From these hexagrams in Betty's casting, it is clear what type of career she should embark upon and how she should bring this change to fruition.

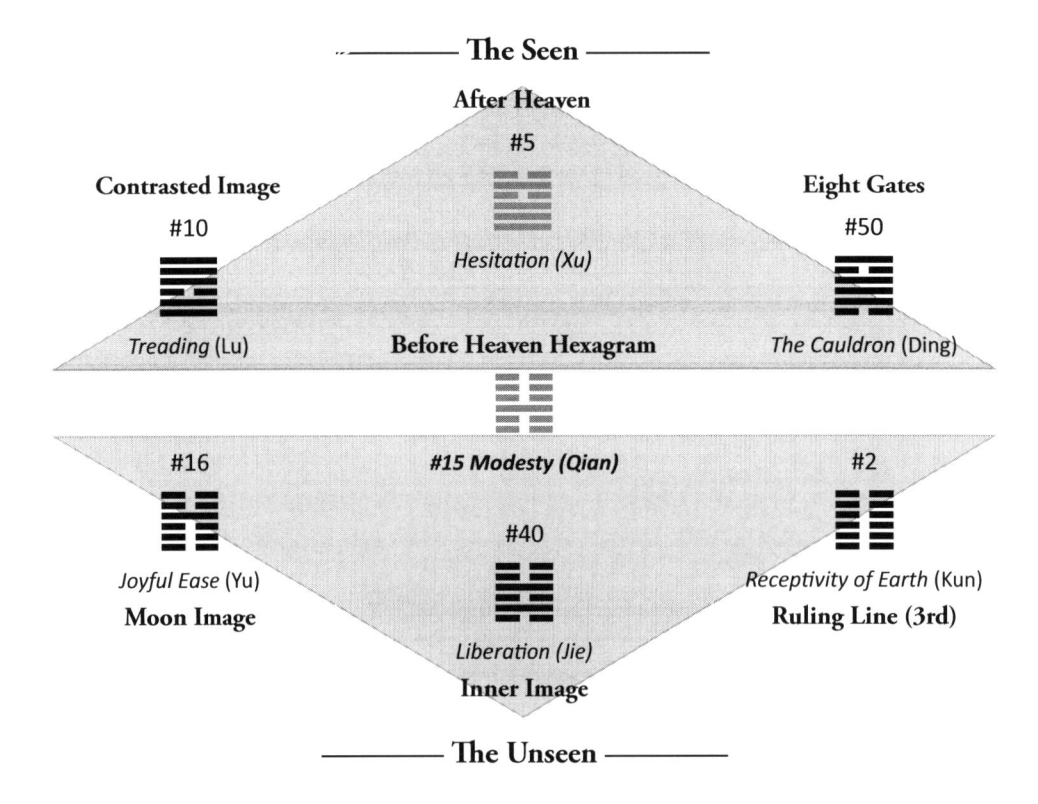

The Seen

After Heaven
#5

Hesitation (Xu)

Contrasted Image
#10

Eight Gates
#50

Treading (Lu)   **Before Heaven Hexagram**   *The Cauldron (Ding)*

#15 Modesty (Qian)

#16

#2

#40

Joyful Ease (Yu)
Moon Image

Receptivity of Earth (Kun)
Ruling Line (3rd)

Liberation (Jie)
Inner Image

The Unseen

The Eight Houses (八房, Ba Fang)

Showing each hexagram within its respective Before Heaven, Contrasted Image, Eight Gates, and After Heaven Houses, and the positions they hold within the house is important not only for reasons of divination, as shown in the previous section, but for calculation as well. There are situations, for example, wherein the *Book of Sun and Moon* can be used in purely a calculative manner, with no manipulation of the stalks, such as determining a person's Eight Characters and Four Pillar Hexagrams. This system of calculation can be applied to many other situations as well, such as planning a business, tracking a stock or investment, determining dates for important events, and so on.

Shao Yong's Before Heaven Eight Houses along with the position of the hexagrams within each house (of which there are eight positions) are crucial in the calculation aspects of the *Book of Sun and Moon*. The Sixty-Four Hexagrams are divided into two main divisions: *Insignia of Yang* (陽儀, Yang Yi) and *Insignia of Yin* (陰儀, Yin Yi).

The Insignia of Yang Division has thirty-two hexagrams and comprises the houses of *Heaven, Valley, Fire,* and *Thunder.* All the first (bottom) lines of these hexagrams are Yang. This Yang Division is then further divided into two sections of sixteen hexagrams, with each of these sections including a subsection of eight hexagrams.

Ultimate Yang Section (太陽, Tai Yang) has sixteen hexagrams with Yang in the first and second lines. These hexagrams comprise the houses of *Heaven* and *Valley*.

#1　#43　#14　#34　#9　#5　#26　#11

The *House of Valley* is subdivided into **Old Yin** (老陰, Lao Yin) because the third lines of these eight hexagrams are all Yin.

#10　#58　#38　#54　#61　#60　#41　#19

Young Yin Section (少陰, Shao Yin) has sixteen hexagrams with Yang in the first lines and Yin in the second lines. These hexagrams comprise the houses of *Fire* and *Thunder*.

#13　#49　#30　#55　#37　#63　#22　#36

The *House of Thunder* is subdivided into **Central Yin** (中陰, Zhong Yin) because the third lines of these eight hexagrams are all Yin.

#25　#17　#21　#51　#42　#3　#27　#24

The Insignia of Yin Division has thirty-two hexagrams and comprises the houses of *Wind, Water, Mountain,* and *Earth*. All the first (bottom) lines of these hexagrams are Yin. This Yin Division is then further divided into two sections of sixteen hexagrams, with each of these sections including a subsection of eight hexagrams.

Young Yang (少陽, Shao Yang) has sixteen hexagrams with Yin in the first lines and Yang in the second lines. These hexagrams comprise the houses of *Wind* and *Water*.

The *House of Wind* is subdivided into **Central Yang** (中陽, Zhong Yang) because the third lines of these eight hexagrams are all Yang.

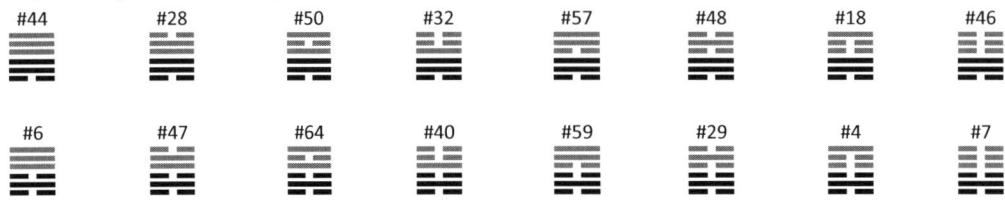

| #44 | #28 | #50 | #32 | #57 | #48 | #18 | #46 |
| #6 | #47 | #64 | #40 | #59 | #29 | #4 | #7 |

Ultimate Yin (太陰, Tai Yin) has sixteen hexagrams wherein all first and second lines are Yin. These hexagrams comprise the houses of *Mountain* and *Earth*.

The *House of Mountain* is subdivided into **Old Yang** (老陽, Lao Yang) because the third lines of these eight hexagrams are all Yang.

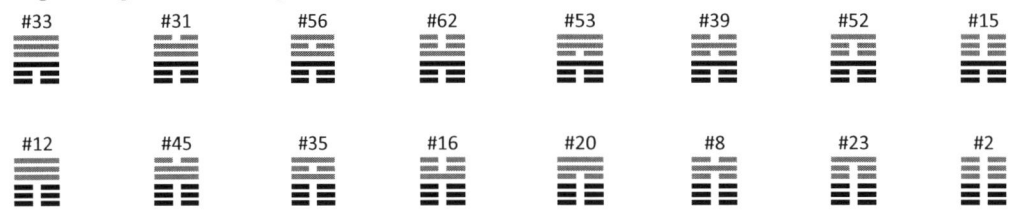

| #33 | #31 | #56 | #62 | #53 | #39 | #52 | #15 |
| #12 | #45 | #35 | #16 | #20 | #8 | #23 | #2 |

From the above designations of the Before Heaven Eight Houses, one can ascertain a great deal of information about any given hexagram. For example, hexagram #46 *Ascending* ䷭ (Earth over Wind) falls under the **Insignia of Yin Division** (showing weakness at the beginning because of its bottom Yin line). It is **Young Yang** (showing it is developing into strength because of its second Yang line), and also **Central Yang** (showing the third Yang line rising up to Yin in the fourth line). It is in the *Fifth House of Wind,* situated in the **eighth position of Earth** (the top trigram is Earth, all Yin lines). Since *Ascending* is in the Before Heaven *House of Wind* it occupies the Southwest direction, showing the **Nine Palace** number is 2 (indicating wealth and livelihood).

A Cross Section of the Before Heaven Sixty-Four Image Illustration

From A Collection on the Essentials of the Rivers He and Luo (河洛精蘊, He Luo Jing Yun).

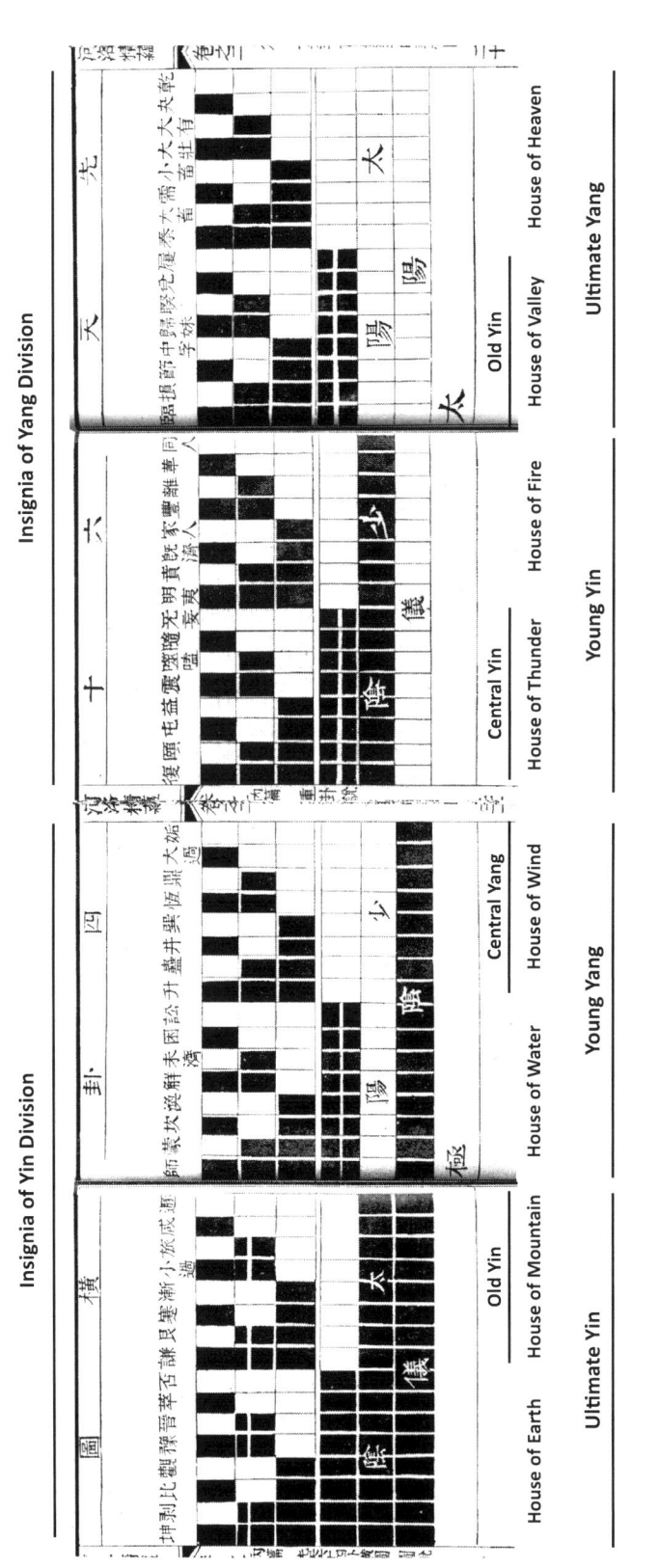

Each square in this illustration counts as one line of a hexagram. The white squares are Yang, and the black squares are Yin. The dashed Yin squares indicate Old Yin lines (which occur in the third line of twenty-four hexagrams) and Central Yin lines (which appear in the fifth line of eight hexagrams). Although these squares are showing a distinction in the type of Yin line, they still represent a single Yin line of the hexagram and should be read accordingly. For example, in the House of Earth, the first column on the left shows six black squares, or lines (with the fifth line being Central Yin). This image, then, reads as six Yin lines, which makes it #2 *Receptivity of Earth*. On the opposite end of the illustration, in the House of Heaven, are six white squares, indicating this as hexagram #1 *Creativity of Heaven*.

Eight House Calculation Method

How is it that the Eight Houses can be used for calculation without the manipulation of the stalks? First, the basis for calculating hexagrams using the Eight Houses is similar to how the Ba Zi calculation is determined. Besides using birth information, you can apply information to any other event as well.

For example, assume you are scheduling a long trip and want to know if it is a safe time to travel, or what you should look out for while traveling.

1) **Time Hexagram:** Determine the Year, Moon, Day, and Time your trip is to occur (if flying, go by ticket times), then check this information to see whether it's an auspicious time for travel. Match this information against your Ba Zi calculation to determine if everything astrologically is aligned and favorable. Determine this Primary Hexagram just as you would in calculating a Life Path Hexagram.

2) **Location Hexagram:** Determine where you are going by looking at the chart on p. 120. Our planet Earth is divided by an Equator (latitude) and a Prime Meridian (longitude), making for four quadrants. There is also the division of latitudes of Tropic of Cancer and Tropic of Capricorn, along with the two Arctic Circles. Together, these total five divisions of the planet Earth, which correspond to the Five Elements (Ten Heavenly Stems). The world is also divided into twenty-four one-hour regions (Chinese use two-hour divisions of time, making for twelve time zones), and these correspond to the Twelve Animal Astrological Signs (Twelve Earthly Branches). By simply lining these coordinates over a map of the world, the corresponding hexagrams of the Sixty-Year Cycle come to represent areas of the world. So, first locate the quadrant you will be traveling to, then determine the more specific area, and from this you will find a hexagram ruling that area. (See also Location Calculations of Dragon Pulses and Hexagrams.)

3) **Event Hexagram:** Taking the upper inner trigram from the Primary Hexagram and the lower inner trigram from the Location Hexagram, a new Event Hexagram is determined. This hexagram will then be used to determine the overall issues of the coming travels and events.

4) **Prediction Hexagram:** From the Event Hexagram, determine the house it belongs to and its position within the house, then count out eight consecutive hexagrams from its position (even if this means counting into the next connected house) to determine the Prediction Hexagram. These eight hexagrams will predict the good fortune or misfortune of events during your travels. From the Prediction Hexagram, you could likewise examine all the Associated Hexagrams and then calculate out each of them according to their house and positions. This process of using the houses and hexagram

positions can become very involved and complex, so it really depends on what information you are seeking and on the importance of the event to be calculated.

Location Calculations of Dragon Pulses and Hexagrams

From very early in Chinese history exists the theory of Dragon movements across the Earth. These geomantic movements took place along specific energy (氣, Qi) pathways or highways, and at the junctures of intersecting lines were what are called *Dragon Pulses* (龍脉, Long Mai). These Dragon Pulses were considered high-energy areas created by geomantic and magnetic influences. The original science of this was called Kan Yu (堪輿), meaning "geomancy," but literally meaning "to cover and support Heaven and Earth," and from this grew the art of Feng Shui (風水, Wind and Water). The idea behind geomancy is that Qi (氣) rides the Wind (風, Feng), but scatters and disperses unless it encounters or is captured by Water (水, Shui). So it is with the idea of a Dragon (emblematic of Qi) moving along geomantic paths of Thunder (stimulation) and Wind (movement). Thus concentrating the Qi (vital energy, Dragon Pulses) in areas of Mountains and Valleys (where water ascends and descends), and so covering and supporting Heaven (sky) and Earth (soil), so the Sun (Li) and Moon (Kan) can function, interact, and move according to Nature's design. From these movements, the functions, connections, and relationships of the Eight Trigrams can be seen with Feng Shui.

This information was presented here to further demonstrate the value of placing hexagrams upon an image of Earth, which is a far simpler method to the more complex imagery of geomantic lines and Dragon Pulse centers, and thus having to calculate these along with the Ten Heavenly Stems and Twelve Earthly Branches to interpret the geomantic influence and locations. Trigrams, as it were, have these correlations and associations built into them and so using hexagrams for location is far less demanding mathematically.

Location by Chinese Astrological Animal Signs

General areas can also be found by using the influences of Chinese Astrological Animal Signs. Since there are twelve animals signs, each is associated with one of the two-hour divisions of time, and since each animal has a Yin and Yang aspect, the twenty-four-hour period is also determined. Thus, the first time zone is calculated with the Rat, and the last time zone is associated with the Pig. Each animal sign has five hexagrams associated with it, according with the Five Elements.

Book of Sun and Moon

Diagram of Earth's Time Zone, Hexagram, Element, and Animal Correspondences

Changing Lines (變爻, Bian Yao)

A Changing Line is derived only during the casting of the Before Heaven Hexagram through the manipulation of the stalks (see Part Eight). Some castings may produce no changing lines, while others could produce as many as six, one for each line of the image. An erroneous view has persisted, at least in the West, that when a Changing Line occurs, the line is then changed, thus creating a new hexagram, and the original casted hexagram is discarded.

Changing Lines are like incidences occurring along one's journey. This is like driving a route from one city to the next, and the Changing Line is like a prediction of some event that will take place somewhere during the journey. So it isn't that the course or destination (Before Heaven Hexagram) has changed, rather some event or situation needs to be addressed before setting out on the journey.

The manner, then, of using and interpreting Changing Lines is not so much about changing the Before Heaven Hexagram as it is about interpreting the Changing Line itself. For example, let's assume the hexagram #20 *Contemplation* (觀, Guan) was cast, and the second line resulted in being a Changing Line, a Yin line changing into a Yang line. When this second line is changed, the hexagram #59 *Dispersion* (渙, Huan) is thus created:

#20 #59

The important aspect of interpreting a Changing Line is just that, interpreting the Changing Line. Meaning, focus on what the Changing Line is in hexagram #20 (second line) and then view that line in image #59 *Dispersion*. In other words, look at the text of the second line of image #20, which reads,

Contemplation by stealing a glance.
Advantageous for the woman to be resolute.

Then go to image #59 and read the second line, which says,

Dispersion is hurried and the opportunity
is seized. Regret vanishes.

The meanings of these lines show not to give your intent away *(by stealing a glance),* and that the situation is beneficial to a female who is determined. From this, what she seeks will come quickly *(Dispersion is hurried)* because she seizes the opportunity without delay and so there is nothing to worry about *(regret vanishes).* In this case, these lines indicate a positive and auspicious outcome. If one focused on the complete images, instead of just these lines in both hexagrams, the idea could possibly be misinterpreted, as *Contemplation* resulting in *Dispersion* has a negative connotation.

There are four fixed rules to follow when dealing with a Changing Line:
1) Read the Changing Line of the casted image and the same-numbered line in the hexagram it creates.
2) Examine the trigrams. In the example above, it shows the lower trigram changing from Earth to Water. This could show, depending on the question asked, that the mother of the situation must seek out the advice or influence of the middle son, or a middle-aged male.
3) Examine the Nine Palace correlations of these two trigrams. Earth is 2 and Water is 1 (in the Lo River Script correlation of Trigrams with Nine Palace numbers). Earth (Kun) is about relationships and love, and Water (Kan) indicates one's livelihood and career. So, for example, this can show that the mother (of this situation) is secretly (stealing a glance) seeking to benefit from some great interest or love of hers, and so seeks out the help of a middle-aged male to further this interest into a career or livelihood.
4) Observe whether the Changing Line is Yin moving to Yang, or Yang moving to Yin. In the preceding example, a Yin line is moving to a Yang line, from a weak position to a strong position.

Obviously, there's much more to properly interpreting a casted hexagram, and the above advice is purely about interpreting a Changing Line. In the event a casting produces more than one Changing Line, follow the above protocols with each Changing Line.

Conclusion

From all this information on how to use the *Yi,* you can see there is great depth to the *Book of Sun and Moon,* but this is hardly a definitive work. In truth, each chapter and subject in this book warrants an entire volume of its own, and this book is just scratching the surface. Having studied and used the *Book of Sun and Moon* since my late teen years, I still feel I haven't come close to reaching its depths. The *Book of Sun and Moon* surely is *The Abyss.*

Using the *Yi* is similar to being a tracker following footprints and signs to determine which way a situation is heading or of how it developed. Within this work, the necessary charts and instructions are given for making good interpretations and tracking of images. Examining all the associated hexagrams developed from a casting gives a much clearer look at what situation is occurring, where it might head toward, and what is generating it.

Part Eight

Casting the Stalks and Ritual for Divination

Daoist Ritual for Casting the Stalks

Creating a Question for the *Yi*

The first consideration is to create a question with no more than eight words or characters. Once a question is created, keep repeating it in your mind during the following ritual and while casting the stalks. The question also needs to be written down on a yellow paper talisman, which will be burnt in the incense urn before casting.

Creating an Altar or Shrine for Casting

This may not have to be a permanent fixture, as after the casting it can be disassembled. The room to be used must be clean and quiet.

Necessary items include:

1) One table large enough to hold an image of Fu Xi and/or King Wen. The table should be covered with a gold or yellow cloth. You can either sit at the table in a chair, or use a low table and sit in a meditation pose for the casting.
2) An incense urn big enough in which to burn the oracle talisman. It's best if juniper incense is used.
3) Flowers.
4) Two red candles.
5) Two plates for fruit offerings (two apples, two oranges, two peaches, and two plums).
6) Five small cups containing pure water, cooked rice, a cooked vegetable, rice wine, and nuts (preferably pine nuts or walnuts).

Casting Talisman

After the altar has been completed, all offerings are in place, and candles lit, recite the *Purifying the Altar Chant* one time. Do so standing or kneeling before the altar. When reciting "Yuan, Heng, Li, and Zhen" face the indicated directions within the chant.

Purifying the Altar Chant

淨壇咒

Jing Tan Zhou

Recite in English:

The pure spirits of Heaven and Earth	天地清靈 Tian Di Qing Ling
are filling this hall with auspicious light.	祥光滿庭 Xiang Guang Man Ting
The dragon on the left and the tiger on the right,	左龍右虎 Zuo Long You Hu
guarding the recitation of the scriptures.	持微誦經 Chi Wei Song Jing
A thousand evils and a myriad of corruptions	千邪萬穢 Qian Xie Wan Hui
are in one sweep cleared away.	一掃而清 Yi Sao Er Qing
Expelling evil ghosts and cutting off evil spirits,	驅除鬼妖 Chu Chu Gui Yao
cutting off all essences of evil,	殄滅邪精 Tian Mie Xie Jing
I take sanctuary in the Great Dao. [Bow]	皈依大道 Gui Yi Da Dao

Recite in Chinese:

    [Face East]

Yuan
    [Bow]

元
Originating

    [Face West]

Heng
    [Bow]

亨
Penetrating

    [Face South]

Li
    [Bow]

利
Advantageous

    [Face North]

Zhen
    [Bow]

貞
Persevering

    [Face altar and recite:]

Wu Feng Xian Shi

吾奉先師
I respectfully make these offerings to all founding ancestors.

Ji Ji Ru Lu Ling
    [Bow]

急急如律令
These mandates I will expediently follow.

The Stalks for Divining

Before the time of King Wen, tortoise shells were heated to produce cracks in the shell and from this the Yin and Yang images were created. Ox shoulder bones were also used for this purpose. At some point, either before or after the time of King Wen, the use of fifty yarrow or milfoil stalks[29] (蓍, Shi) became the sacred implement of divination for the *Yi*. It was also considered acceptable and auspicious to use the stalks of the plant Heavenly Bamboo (天竹, Tian Zhu, or its Latin name, Nandina domestica), of which the stalks are very similar in size to those of the yarrow.

The older method for casting the hexagrams, the yarrow stalk method, was gradually replaced during the Han Dynasty by the three coins method and the yarrow stalk method was lost. With the coin method, the probability of Yin or Yang is equal while with the recreated yarrow stalk method of Zhu Xi (朱熹, 1130–1200 CE), the probability of old Yang is three times greater than old Yin.

Several references to the stalks occur in the *Ten Wings*. In the ninth chapter of the *Upper Great Appendix* of the *Ten Wings* the following statement concerns the use of the stalks:

> The numbers of the Great Expanse is 50, but only 49 of these are used. The stalks are then divided into two piles to represent the sets of the two emblems [Heaven and Earth, Sun and Moon]. One stalk is then taken [from the right pile] and placed [in the left hand] and this symbolizes the Three [Heaven, Humanity, and Earth].
> 大衍之數五十,其用四十有九,分而為二以象兩,掛一以象三.
> Da Yan Zhi Shu Wu Shi, Qi Yong Si Shi You Jiu, Fen Er Wei Er Yi Xiang Liang, Gua Yi Yi Xiang San.

In chapter 1 on the *Treatise of Remarks on the Trigrams*, it says,

> In antiquity, the sages composed the *Yi* so the Illuminated Spirits could give them mystical assistance, and so from this came about the creation of the stalks.
> 昔者聖人之作易也.幽贊於神明而生蓍.
> Xi Zhe Sheng Ren Zhi Zuo Yi Ye. You Zan Yu Shen Ming Er Sheng Shi.

---

[29] Achillea millefolium has leaves resembling those of ferns with broad, flat-like clusters of flowering heads. The dried stalks of this plant are cut into approximately six- to thirteen-inch lengths.

Divination Using the Stalks

Within the *Ten Wings* it states that only tortoise shells and yarrow stalks are approved by the spirits for divination via the *Yi*. Obviously, no one nowadays should consider using tortoise shells. Besides the issues of animal cruelty involved in removing and heating tortoise shells, no clear records exist on how to do it properly or on how to interpret the results. However, the methods for manipulating the stalks for divination are not only effective and easy to follow, but no animals are harmed in the process.

Ideally, the fifty stalks should be made from either yarrow (milfoil) or some type of bamboo, preferably Heavenly Bamboo. They should be anywhere from one to two feet in length. When not in use, wrap the stalks in a clean silk cloth and store them in some sort of decorative box or case. Place the box or case on a clean shelf set above or equal to shoulder height. This shows respect for the *Yi*.

After performing the *Yi Spirit Daoist Ritual*, cast the stalks as follows:

Preparation

Pass the fifty stalks through the incense smoke three times, then immediately remove one stalk and place it in the storage receptacle (you will no longer need this stalk throughout the procedure). This will then leave a remainder of forty-nine stalks.

Note: Always ensure you have exactly fifty stalks before starting, otherwise the calculation procedure will be in vain.

First Sorting

Step One: Turn and rub the stalks between the palms of both hands nine times. Then, holding the stalks in the right hand, stretch out the right arm and with the thumb divide the stalks into two groups. Bring the right arm back and then use both hands to separate the groups completely and place them on the table into two piles. The left-hand pile represents the Sun/Yang side, and the right-hand grouping represents the Moon/Yin portion.

Step Two: With the right hand, take one stalk from the Sun pile and place it between the little and ring fingers of the left hand.

Step Three: With the right-hand fingers, push away four stalks at a time from the Sun pile until there is a remainder of either one, two, three, or four stalks. Pick up the remainder with the right hand and place it between the ring finger and middle finger of the left hand.

Step Four: Again with the right hand, push away four stalks at a time, but this time, from the Moon pile until there remains either one, two, three, or four stalks. Pick up this remainder with the right hand and place it between the middle finger and index finger of the left hand.

Note: After becoming familiar with casting, you will know how many stalks to pull from the Moon pile without having to divide it by fours. Since the remaining number of stalks from this first sorting can only be five or nine, you need only know how many stalks you have from the Sun pile to determine what to pull from the Moon pile. Remember, this number includes the one stalk you place between your little and ring fingers. So, if you end up with less than five total from the Sun pile, you need only pull the proper number from the Moon pile to give you five stalks. This will either be one, two, or three stalks. If, however, you have five stalks in your left hand after Step Three (one between the little and ring fingers plus four between the ring and middle fingers) then you have to pull four stalks from the Moon pile because the total remainder of stalks from both piles has to then equal nine (five from the Sun pile and four from the Moon pile).

Step Five: Group the five or nine stalks that are in your left hand and set them aside on the table.

Second Sorting

Step Six: Bunch together the sorted stalks from both the Sun and Moon piles, rub them between the hands nine times, stretch out the right hand holding the stalks, and divide them with the right thumb. Bring the right hand back and with both hands separate the stalks and place them into Sun and Moon piles again.

Step Seven: Again, take one stalk from the Sun pile and place it between the little finger and ring finger of your left hand.

Step Eight: Again, push away four stalks at a time from the Sun pile until only one, two, three, or four stalks remain. Place the remaining stalks between the ring finger and middle finger of your left hand.

Step Nine: Next, with the right hand push away four stalks at a time from the Moon pile until one, two, three, or four stalks remain. Place the remainder between the middle finger and index finger of your left hand.

Step Ten: In your left hand there can only be either four or eight stalks. These are then grouped together and set aside on the table. Set them a little apart from the stalks of the first sorting.

Third Sorting

Step Eleven: Bunch together all the sorted stalks together, rub them between the hands, stretch out the right hand holding the stalks, divide them with the right thumb. Bring the right hand back and with both hands separate the stalks and place them into two piles.

Step Twelve: Again, take one stalk from the Sun pile and place it between the little and ring fingers of your left hand.

Step Thirteen: Again, push away four stalks at a time from the Sun pile until only one, two, three, or four stalks remain. Place the remaining stalks between the ring and middle fingers of your left hand.

Step Fourteen: Next, with the right hand push away four stalks at a time from the Moon pile until one, two, three, or four stalks remain, then place the remainder between the middle and index fingers of your left hand.

Step Fifteen: Again, as in the Second Sorting there can only be either four or eight stalks in your left hand. Group these together and set them on the table, a little apart from the stalks of the first and second sortings.

Now, using the table on p. 130, determine, from the three piles the three numbers of stalks in them. For example, if the three piles come to 9 + 8 + 4, this means the line is a Young Yang line and is unchanging. It is always a good idea to write the numbers down in case the piles get mixed up.

From the above procedures you have now derived the first (bottom line) of the pending hexagram image. For each successive line, perform the same methods of three sorting stages until all six lines are created.

Table for Determining the Lines:

5 + 4 + 4 = Old Yang Line (Changing Line)
9 + 8 + 8 = Old Yin Line (Changing Line)

5 + 8 + 8 = Young Yang Line (Unchanging Line)
9 + 8 + 4 = Young Yang Line (Unchanging Line)
9 + 4 + 8 = Young Yang Line (Unchanging Line)

5 + 4 + 8 = Young Yin Line (Unchanging Line)
5 + 8 + 4 = Young Yin Line (Unchanging Line)
9 + 4 + 4 = Young Yin Line (Unchanging Line)

Once the first line is created and determined, bring all forty-nine stalks back together in one pile again and proceed from Step Two through Step Fifteen. For each line there are Three Sortings, with a total of six lines to be created, this means a total of eighteen procedures must take place.

When all six lines have been cast, refer to the Chart for Determining Hexagrams on p. 136 to see which of the Sixty-Four Hexagrams was created. The trigrams on the vertical (left) side represent the bottom trigram of the hexagram (lines 1, 2, and 3). The horizontal row of trigrams at the top represent the upper trigrams (lines 4, 5, and 6). From connecting the appropriate upper and lower trigrams, the casted hexagram will be determined.

Suggested Reading

Bibliography of English Books

I Ching Coin Prediction: How to Consult the I Ching to Predict Your Future by Da Liu (Harper & Row Publishers, 1975).

I Ching Numerology: Based on Shao Yung's Classic Plum Blossom Numerology by Da Liu (Harper & Row, San Francisco, 1979).

I Ching: The Book of Changes and the Unchanging Truth, Revised Edition by Hua-Ching Ni (SevenStar Communications Group, Inc., 1983).

I Ching: The Book of Change by John Blofeld (Dutton/Plume, 1968).

I Ching: The Classic Chinese Oracle of Change. Translated by Stephen Karcher (Vega, 2002).

The Astrology of I Ching. Translated from the 'Ho Map Lo Map Rational Number' Manuscript by W. K. Chu. Edited, and commentaries added, by W. A. Sherrill (Penguin Books, 1993).

The Classic of Changes: A New Translation of the I Ching as Interpreted by Wang Bi. Translated by Richard John Lynn (Columbia University Press, 2004).

The Complete I Ching by Taoist Master Alfred Huang (Inner Traditions International, 1998).

The I Ching Book of Changes. Translated by James Legge, edited with an introduction and study guide by Ch'u Chai with Winberg Chai (Bantam Books, 1986).

The I Ching, or, Book of Changes (Bollingen Series XIX) by Richard Wilhelm and Cary F. Baynes (Princeton University Press; 3rd edition, 1967).

The Original I Ching Oracle by Rudolf Ritsema and Shantena Augusto Sabbadini (Watkins Publishing, 2005).

The Taoist I Ching. Translated by Thomas Cleary (Shambala Publications, Inc., 1986).

The Text of Yi King: (and Its Appendixes) Chinese Original With English Translation by Z. D. Sung (The China Modern Education Company, 1935).

Bibliography of Chinese Texts

河洛精蘊, He Lou Jing Yun. *A Collection on the Essentials of the Rivers He and Luo*, Four volumes, early Qing dynasty work (Reprinted by White Cloud Monastery, 1989).

周易異文考, Zhou Yi Yi Wen Kao. *The Book of Changes of Zhou Literary Explanation* (China, 1964).

六十四卦經解, 朱駿聲, Liu Shi Si Gua Jing Jie, Zhu Jun. *An Explanation of the Sixty-Four Images Classic* by Zhu Junsheng (China, 1960).

最新八字推命哲學, 臥龍泰仙著, Zui Xin Ba Zi Tui Ming Zhe Xue, Wo Long Tai Xian Zhe. *A New Philosophical Advancement on Determining Destiny Through the Ba Zi* (China, 1906).

中華周易, Zhong Hua Zhou Yi. *China's Zhou Dynasty Book of Change* (No publisher or date listed, China).

周易參同契考異, 未拍陽著, Zhou Yi Can Tong Qi, Wei Poyang Zhe. *The Zhou Yi Cantong Qi Clarified by Wei Poyang* (No publisher or date listed, China).

太極拳圖說, Tai Ji Quan Tu Shuo. *Tai Ji Quan Illustrated and Explained* by Chen Pinsan, edited by Chen Panling (Taipei, 1953).

About the Author

Stuart Alve Olson, long-time protégé of Master T.T. Liang (1900–2002), is a teacher, translator, and writer on Daoist philosophy, health, and internal arts. Since the early 1970s, he has studied and practiced Daoism and Chinese Buddhism. As of 2014, Stuart has published twenty books, many of which now appear in several foreign-language editions.

Daoism Books

- *The Immortal: True Accounts of the 250-Year-Old Man, Li Qingyun* by Yang Sen (Valley Spirit Arts, 2014).
- *Being Daoist: The Way of Drifting With the Current* (Valley Spirit Arts, 2014)
- *The Jade Emperor's Mind Seal Classic: The Taoist Guide to Health, Longevity, and Immortality* (Inner Traditions, 2003).
- *Tao of No Stress: Three Simple Paths* (Healing Arts Press, 2002).
- *Qigong Teachings of a Taoist Immortal: The Eight Essential Exercises of Master Li Ching-Yun* (Healing Arts Press, 2002).

Forthcoming

- *Clarity and Tranquility: A Daoist Guide on the Meditation Practice of Tranquil Sitting.*
- *Refining the Elixir: The Internal Alchemy Teachings of Daoist Immortal Zhang Sanfeng* (Daoist Immortal Three Peaks Zhang Series).
- *Seen and Unseen: A Daoist Guide for the Meditation Practice of Inner Contemplation.*
- *The Yellow Emperor's Yin Convergence Scripture.*
- *The Actions and Retribution Treatise.*

Taijiquan Books

Chen Kung Series

- *Tai Ji Qi: Fundamentals of Qigong, Meditation, and Internal Alchemy,* vol. 1 (Valley Spirit Arts, 2013).
- *Tai Ji Jin: Discourses on Intrinsic Energies for Mastery of Self-Defense Skills,* vol. 2 (Valley Spirit Arts, 2013).
- *Tai Ji Bing Shu: Discourses on the Taijiquan Weapon Arts of Sword, Saber, and Staff,* vol. 6 (Valley Spirit Arts, 2014).

Forthcoming Books in Chen Kung Series

- *Tai Ji Quan: Practice and Philosophy of the 108-Posture Solo Form,* vol. 3 (Valley Spirit Arts, 2015).

- *Tai Ji Tui Shou & Da Lu: Mastering the Eight Operations of Sensing Hands and Greater Rolling-Back,* vol. 4 (Valley Spirit Arts, 2015).
- *Tai Ji San Shou: Dispersing Hands Exercises for Mastering Intrinsic Energies Skills,* vol. 5 (Valley Spirit Arts, 2015).

- *Tai Ji Quan Treatise: Attributed to the Song Dynasty Daoist Priest Zhang Sanfeng,* Daoist Immortal Three Peaks Zhang Series (Valley Spirit Arts, 2011).
- *Imagination Becomes Reality: 150-Posture Taijiquan of Master T.T. Liang* (Valley Spirit Arts, 2011).
- *The Wind Sweeps Away the Plum Blossoms: Yang Style Taijiquan Staff and Spear Techniques* (Valley Spirit Arts, 2011).
- *Steal My Art: The Life and Times of Tai Chi Master T.T. Liang* (North Atlantic Books, 2002).
- *T'ai Chi According to the I Ching—Embodying the Principles of the Book of Changes* (Healing Arts Press, 2002).
- *T'ai Chi for Kids: Move with the Animals,* illustrated by Gregory Crawford (Bear Cub Books, 2001).

Kung-Fu
- *The Complete Guide to Northern Praying Mantis Kung Fu* (Blue Snake Books, 2010).

  Forthcoming
  - *18 Lohan Exercises* (Valley Spirit Arts, 2015).

Check out Stuart's author page at Amazon:
www.amazon.com/author/stuartalveolson

About the Publisher

Valley Spirit Arts offers books and DVDs on Daoism, taijiquan, and meditation practices primarily from author Stuart Alve Olson, longtime student of Master T.T. Liang and translator of many Daoist-related works.

Its website provides teachings on meditation and internal alchemy, taijiquan, qigong, and kung fu through workshops, private and group classes, and online courses and consulting.

For more information as well as updates on Stuart Alve Olson's upcoming projects and events, please visit: www.valleyspiritarts.com

About the Sanctuary of Dao

Established in 2010, the Sanctuary of Dao is a nonprofit organization dedicated to the sharing of Daoist philosophy and practices through online resources, yearly meditation retreats, and community educational programs. The underlying mission of the Sanctuary of Dao is to bring greater health, longevity, and contentment to its members and everyone it serves.

Please visit www.sanctuaryofdao.org for more information about the organization and its programs.

Chart for Determining Hexagrams

Trigrams Upper / Lower	Qian	Dui	Li	Zhen	Xun	Kan	Gen	Kun
Qian	#1 Creativity of Heaven	#43 Decision	#14 Great Possession	#34 Great Strength	#9 Small Accumulation	#5 Hesitation	#26 Great Accumulation	#11 Peacefulness
Dui	#10 Treading	#58 Joyousness	#38 Opposition	#54 Marriageable Maiden	#61 Inner Truth	#60 Regulating	#41 Sacrifice	#19 Approaching
Li	#13 People United	#49 Revolution	#30 Distant Brightness	#55 Prosperity	#37 The Family	#63 After Completion	#22 Adornment	#36 Diminishing Light
Zhen	#25 Innocence	#17 Following	#21 Mastication	#51 Arousing Movement	#42 Increase	#3 Beginning Difficulties	#27 Nourishment	#24 Returning
Xun	#44 Pairing	#28 Great Passing	#50 The Cauldron	#32 Constancy	#57 Submission	#48 The Well	#18 Inner Destruction	#46 Ascending
Kan	#6 Contending	#47 Oppression	#64 Before Completion	#40 Liberation	#59 Dispersion	#29 The Abyss	#4 Untaught Youth	#7 The Army
Gen	#33 Retreating	#31 Attraction	#56 The Wanderer	#62 Small Passing	#53 Gradual Movement	#39 Difficult Obstruction	#52 Determined Stillness	#15 Modesty
Kun	#12 Adversity	#45 Collecting	#35 Advancement	#16 Joyful Ease	#20 Contemplation	#8 Union	#23 Removing	#2 Receptivity of Earth

Made in the USA
Middletown, DE
07 June 2015